SOLUTIONS MANUAL FOR FINANCIAL LITERACY

Introduction to the Mathematics of Interest, Annuities, and Insurance

Kenneth Kaminsky

University Press of America,® Inc.
Lanham · Boulder · New York · Toronto · Oxford

4501 Forbes Boulevard
Suite 200
Lanham, Maryland 20706
UPA Acquisitions Department (301) 459-3366

PO Box 317
Oxford
OX2 9RU, UK

Printed in the United States of America
British Library Cataloging in Publication Information Available

ISBN: 978-0-7618-2623-1

™ The paper used in this publication meets the minimum requirements of American National Standard for Information Sciences—Permanence of Paper for Printed Library Materials, ANSI Z39.48—1984

Table of Contents

Chapter 1

Exercises 1.2

1.2.1 January 1, 2002 is 226 years. At the annual interest rate of 2.5%, \$4,000 becomes $\$4{,}000(1.025)^{226} \approx \$1{,}060{,}849$.

1.2.2 The assurance means that $\$15{,}000(1+i)^{2.5} = \$30{,}000$. Thus, $i = (\$30{,}000/\$15{,}000)^{1/2.5} - 1 = .3195079\ldots = 31.95079\ldots\%$.

1.2.3 If the initial value of the work was V, it has increased in value in n years to $1.5V$ at the rate of 12% per year. This means that $V(1.12)^n = 1.5V$. The V's cancel giving $(1.12)^n = 1.5$ and finally, $n = \log(1.5)/\log(1.12) = 3.57778\ldots$ years. That's almost 3 years and 7 months.

1.2.4 Faramarz is looking for P so that $P(1.06)^4 = \$10{,}000$ giving $P = \$10{,}000(1.06)^{-4} \approx \$7{,}920.94$.

1.2.5 a) José Luis's \$500 grows to $\$500(1+i)^3 = \$750$ in three years at annual interest rate i. This gives $i = (\$750/\$500)^{1/3} - 1 = .14471\ldots \approx 14.471\%$.

b) In five years José Luis has $\$500(1.14471\ldots)^5 \approx \$982.78$.

1.2.6 a) Sukie's investment grew from \$11,000 to \$14,500 in three years at annual rate i. Thus $\$11{,}000(1+i)^3 = \$14{,}500$ so $i = (\$14{,}500/\$11{,}000)^{1/3} - 1 = .096457\ldots = 9.6457\ldots\%$

b) One year from now is two years since it reached \$14,500, so in one year Sukie's investment will be worth $\$14{,}500 \cdot (1.096457\ldots)^2 = \$17{,}432.17$.

1.2.7 Sita's money will be worth $\$6{,}000(1+i)^{10} = \$24{,}000$ in 10 years. This means that i must be $i = (\$32{,}000/\$6{,}000)^{1/10} - 1 = .148698\ldots = 14.8698\ldots\%$.

1.2.8 Barbro will have $\$12{,}000(1.0784)^5 \approx \$17{,}501.72$. That's \$1.72 more than she needs.

1.2.9 Joanna's money has been exposed to interest for 1,760 days = 1,760/365.25 years = 4.8186... years. Her \$500 has grown to $\$500(1+i)^{4.8186\ldots} = \$698.18$. This gives

$$i = (\$698.18/\$500)^{1/4.8186\ldots} - 1 = .071744\ldots\ 7.1744\ldots\%.$$

1.2.10 Shimon borrowed $P = \$4{,}130.35(1.085)^{-3} \approx \$3{,}233.68$.

1.2.11 If true the interest rate i satisfies $P(1 + i)^{0.5} = 2P$. The P's cancel so $i = 2^{1/0.5} - 1 = 3 = 300\%$.

Exercises 1.3

1.3.4 Here is a time diagram for the situation.

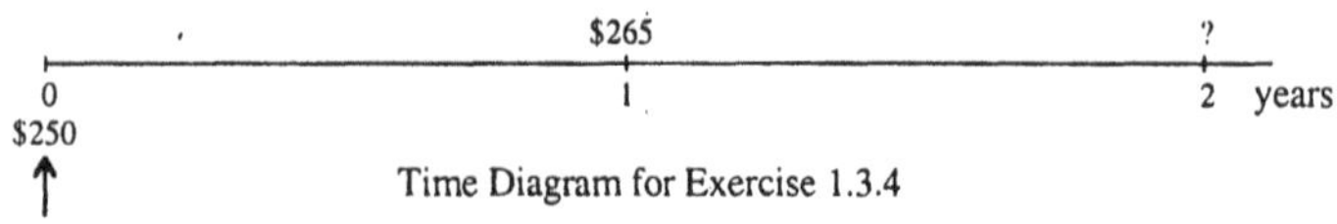

Time Diagram for Exercise 1.3.4

We first find the interest rate that Samantha's sister was charging. That rate satisfies $\$250(1 + i) = \$265$, so $i = 6\%$. To repay her loan in two years, Samantha should pay $P = \$250(1.06)^2 = \$280.90$.

1.3.5 Below is a time diagram for Joel's situation. Again we need the interest rate being charged.

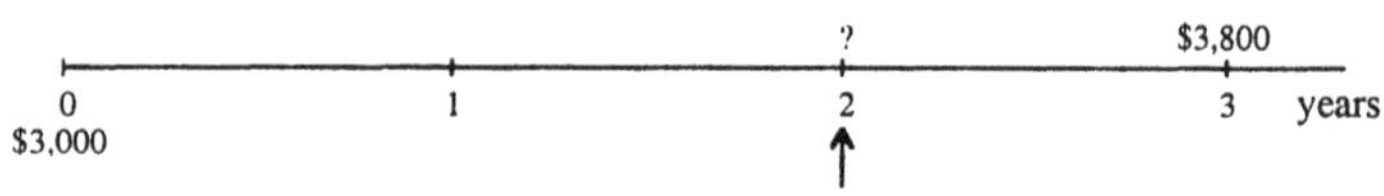

Time Diagram for Exercise 1.3.5

We have $\$3{,}000(1 + i)^3 = \$3{,}800$ which yields $i = (\$3{,}800/\$3{,}000)^{1/3} - 1 = .08198\ldots$ But Joel will pay after two years so he should pay $P = \$3{,}000(1.08198\ldots)^2 = \$3{,}512.07$.

1.3.6 Below is a time diagram for Freddie's transaction. The interest rate must satisfy $\$10{,}000(1 + i)^{10} = \$21{,}560.19$ from which we get $i = .0798545\ldots$

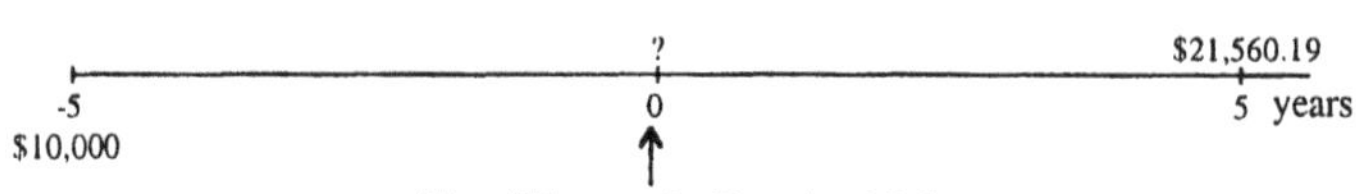

Time Diagram for Exercise 1.3.6

Freddie's balance at time 0 is $\$10{,}000(1.0798545\ldots)^5 = \$14{,}683.39$.

1.3.7 This is an interesting problem because we don't know i or n, and we don't need to. We are just going to need $(1 + i)^n$. From time n years to time $2n$ years, n years have passed so that we have the equation of value $\$12{,}094.47(1 + i)^n = \$18{,}298.76$ which gives $(1 + i)^n = 1.51298\ldots$ From the time diagram below you see that $P(1+i)^n = P(1.51298...) = \$12,094.47$, so $P = \$7,993.78$.

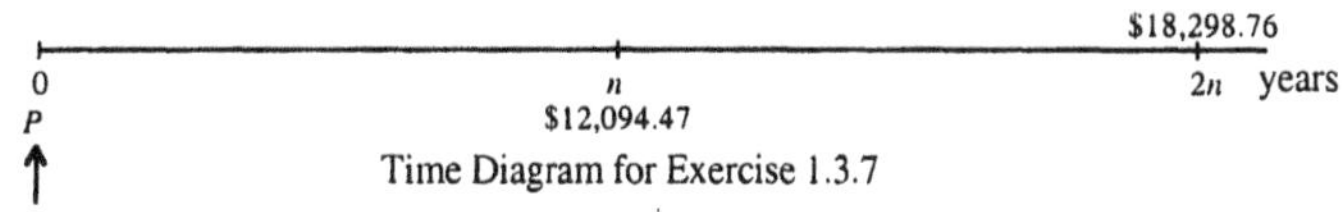

Time Diagram for Exercise 1.3.7

1.3.8 We can find the interest rate from the equivalence of \$3,200 in 3 years and \$4,000 in 4 years. From $\$3,200(1+i) = \$4,000$ we solve for i to get $i = 25\%$. Then, the amount borrowed is $L = \$4,000(1.25)^{-4} = \$1,638.40$.

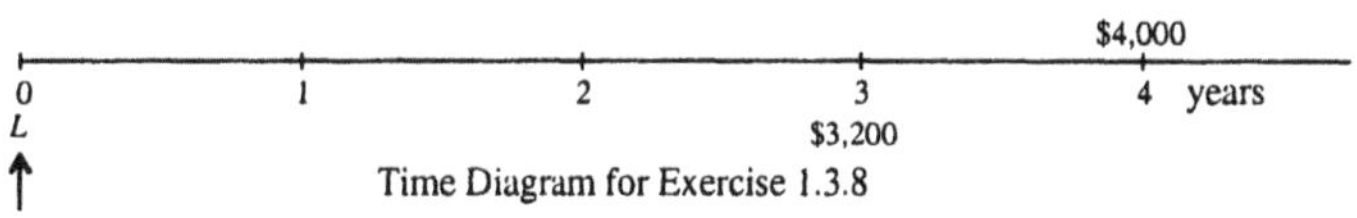

Time Diagram for Exercise 1.3.8

1.3.9 We can write $\$30,000 = \$22,500(1.08)^n$ and solve for n. We find $n = \log(1.\overline{3})/\log(1.08) \approx 3.738$ years before the \$30,000 payment. The earlier date is 5 - 3.738 = 1.262 years after time zero.

1.3.10 At time 0, the \$30,000 payment is worth $\$30,000(1.08)^{-5} = \$20,417.50$.

1.3.11 The time diagram below will serve for the whole problem. Move the arrow from -6, to 0 to +4 for parts a), b), and c) respectively.

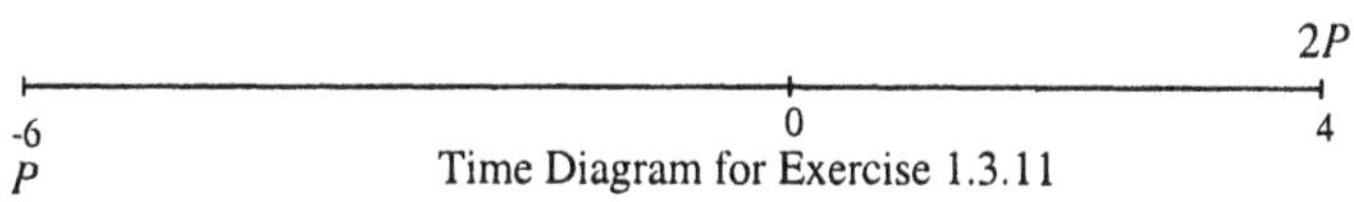

Time Diagram for Exercise 1.3.11

a) With the focal date at -6, we equate P with the value of $2P$ discounted 10 years. That is, $P = 2P(1+i)^{-10}$.
b) Now, move the arrow to 0. We equate the value of P accumulated 6 years with the value of $2P$ discounted 4 years. We get $P(1+i)^6 = 2P(1+i)^{-4}$.
c) If the focal date is four years from now, we equate the value of P accumulated 10 years with $2P$. This gives $P(1+i)^{10} = 2P$.
d) For each of the three equations of value, divide both sides by P and solve for $1+i$. In each case we get $1+i = 2^{1/10}$.

Solving for i gives $i = .07177... \approx 7.177\%$.

1.3.12 We could use either Formula 1.1 or 1.2 for this. I put the arrow at 2 years in the time diagram below, so Formula 1.1 it is. The

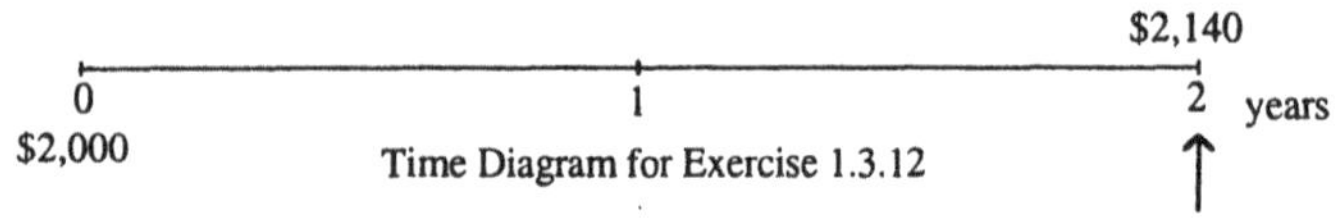

Time Diagram for Exercise 1.3.12

equation of value is $\$200(1 + i)^2 = \$214$, or $(1 + i)^2 = 214/210 = 1.07$, so $1 + i = (1.07)^{1/2} = 1.034408...$, and $i = 1.034408... - 1 = .034408... \approx 3.4408\%$.

1.3.13 Since each \$1 is to become \$2, we need to find n so that $(1.06)^n = 2$. Using the Log Rule, we find $n = \log(2)/\log(1.06) \approx 11.89566...$ years.

1.3.14 First, we need to find out what interest rate Frema was to earn the first year. This amount is $i = (4{,}220/4{,}000)^{1/1} - 1 = .055 = 5.5\%$. This is from Formula 1.3.

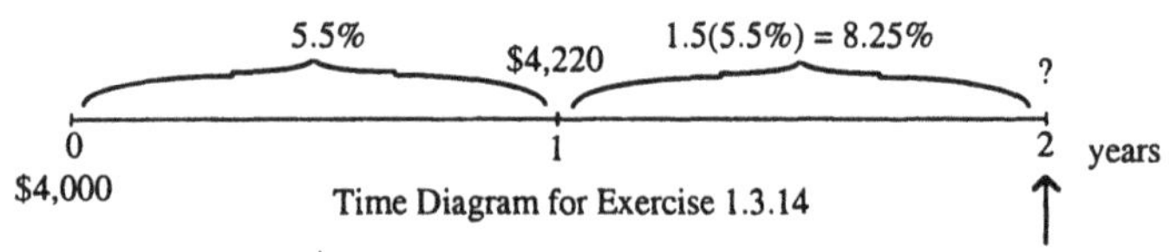

Time Diagram for Exercise 1.3.14

Ewan must pay a 50% higher rate the second year. This amount is 1.5(5.5%) = 8.25%. With the help of the time diagram below, we can write \$4,220(1.0825) = \$4,568.15. Note that this may also have been written \$4,000·(1.055)·(1.0825) = \$4,568.15.

Exercises 1.4

1.4.1 We are looking for δ for which $\$2{,}499(1 - \delta)^3 = \$945$. The solution is $\delta = 1 - (\$945/\$2{,}499)^{1/3} = .27686... = 27.686\%$.

1.4.2 Here the equation of value is $\$3{,}040(1 - .35)^n = \$750$ and it is n that we don't know. Solving for n we get $n = \log(\$750/\$3{,}040)/\log(1 - .35) = 3.249$ years $\approx$ 3 years, 3 months.

1.4.3 This is best shown in a table:

Year No.	*% Lost*	*Rate of Depreciation*	*Current Value*
0	-	-	\$1,499.00
1	32	1 - .32 = .68	\$1,019.32
2	16	1 - .16 = .84	\$856.23
3	8	1 - .08 = .92	\$787.73
4	4	1 - .04 = .96	**\$756.22**

1.4.4 What we know is that $\$134{,}500(1 - \delta)^5 = \$10{,}400$ which tells us that $1 - \delta = (\$10{,}400/\$134{,}500)^{1/5} = .59932\ldots$ What we then want is $\$134{,}500(1 - \delta)^3 = \$134{,}500(.59932\ldots)^3 =$ \$28,954.02.

1.4.5 a) In 6 years the population has gone from 21,139,656 to 12,171,974 by equal annual percentage decreases. We can write $21{,}139{,}656(1 - \delta)^6 = 12{,}171{,}974$ giving $1 - \delta = (12{,}171{,}974/21{,}139{,}656)^{1/6} = .91210\ldots$ It's another 4 years to the present so the current population is $12{,}171{,}974 \cdot (.91210\ldots)^4 = 8{,}424{,}350$.

b) The annual rate of decrease is $\delta = 1 - .91210\ldots = 087897\ldots = 8.7897\ldots\%$.

1.4.6 Given $D = B(1 - \delta)^n$ the solution for B is $B = D/(1 - \delta)^n = D(1 - \delta)^{-n}$. To find the solution for δ we get in turn $(1 - \delta)^n = D/B$, $1 - \delta = (D/B)^{1/n}$, and finally, $\delta = 1 - (D/B)^{1/n}$. To find the solution for n we get in turn $(1 - \delta)^n = D/B$, and $n = \log(D/B)/\log(1 - \delta)$.

1.4.7 a) From $\$985(1 - \delta)^{10} = \$150$ we have in turn $(1 - \delta)^{10} = \$150/\$985$; $(1 - \delta) = (\$150/\$985)^{1/10}$; and $\delta = 1 - (\$150/\$985)^{1/10} = .17155\ldots = 17.155\ldots\%$.

b) In 5 years, the saw will be worth $\$985(1 - .17155\ldots)^5 =$ \$384.38.

1.4.8 If the machine loses 40% each year, it retains 60% of its value each year. Thus, after 4 years, the value of Lasse's machine is $\$345(.6)^4 = \$44.71$.

1.4.9 In 6 years the car will be worth $\$31{,}280(1 - .15)^6 = \$11{,}797.24$.

1.4.10 After n years the printer is worth $\$2345(1 - .2)^n$. The values for the first 5 years are given in the table below:

Year	*Value*
1	$1,876.00
2	$1,500.80
3	$1,200.64
4	$960.51
5	$768.41

Chapter 2

Exercises 2.1

2.1.1 The entries in the second column are found from $1,000·$(1 + .08/m)^{5m}$. The missing entries are in bold.

Number of Compoundings per year, m	*Accumulated value of $1,000 at 8% after 5 years, with compounding m times per year*
1	**$1,469.33**
2	$1,480.24
4	**$1,485.95**
12	$1,489.85
365	**$1,491.76**
8,760 (hourly)	**$1,491.82**

2.1.2 a) At $j_1 = 6\%$ the deposit was $20,000$(1.06)^{-21}$ = $5,883.11.
b) At $j_2 = 8\%$ the deposit was $20,000$(1 + .08/2)^{-42}$ = $3,851.50.
c) At $j_{12} = 12\%$ the deposit was $20,000$(1 + .12/12)^{-252}$ = $1,629.46.

2.1.3 We'll write t for the number of years. Then $4t$ is the number of quarters. The equation of value is $\$45,000\left(1+\frac{.114}{4}\right)^{4t} = \$135,000$ which must be solved for t. We get $4t$ = log(3)/log(1.0285) = 39.095... quarters, or t = 9.774... years.

2.1.4 Mimi's account, 145 years later, is worth $\$200\left(1+\frac{.0275}{4}\right)^{4\times145} = \$10,637.84$.

2.1.5 Compounding daily Helen has $\$10,000\left(1+\frac{.05}{365}\right)^{365} = \$10,512.67$ in one year. With hourly compounding Helen would have $\$10,000\left(1+\frac{.05}{365\times24}\right)^{365\times24} = \$10,512.71$ in one year.

2.1.6 If j_2 is the nominal annual rate compounded semi-annually then we can write the equation of value $P\left(1+\frac{j_2}{2}\right)^{5\times 2} = 2P$. Canceling the P's and solving for j_2 we get $j_2 = 2(2^{1/10} - 1) = .1435469\ldots = 14.35469\ldots\%$. To find when Valerie's money will triple, write n for the number of years and $2n$ for the number of half-years. Then $P(1+\frac{.1435469\ldots}{2})^{2n} = 3P$. The solution is $2n = 15.84962\ldots$, so $n = 7.9248\ldots$ years. That's 7.9248... years from the time of the investment, or 2.9248 years from now.

2.1.7 Astrid's accumulated value after 2 years at 10% is $\$10{,}000\left(1+\frac{.1}{m}\right)^{2m}$, where m is the number of compoundings per year. Here are the results for m = 1, 12, 365, 8760 in a table:

Part	*Number m*	*Accumulation*
a)	1	\$12,100.00
b)	12	\$12,203.91
c)	365	\$12,213.69
d)	8,760	\$12,214.01

2.1.8 Jesper's \$5,000 becomes $\$5{,}000\left(1+\frac{.096}{12}\right)^{3\times 12} = \$6{,}661.15$, so the interest he earned was \$6,661.15 - \$5,000 = \$1,661.15.

2.1.9 Nat invested P where $P\left(1+\frac{.12}{6}\right)^{10\times 6} = \$121{,}719.74$, so P = \$37,098.02.

2.1.10 The equation of value for Björn's investment is $\$15{,}000\left(1+\frac{.085}{2}\right)^{2\times n} = \$30{,}000$, where n is measured in years. Solving for n gives $n = 8.326\ldots$ years.

2.1.11 We have $\$131{,}119.78 = \$100{,}000\left(1+\frac{i}{12}\right)^{3\times 12}$, which implies that $i \approx 9.065440116\%$.

Exercises 2.2

2.2.1. See the time diagram below. Ignore the \$4,300 for part a).

a) The equation of value for the annual payment is $\$4{,}000 = P(1.04)^{-1} + P(1.04)^{-2} + P(1.04)^{-3} = P(2.775091\ldots)$ from which we get $P = \$1{,}441.39$.

b) We don't know where to put the \$4,300 payment. Call the time t. What we do know is that $\$4{,}000(1.04)^t = \$4{,}300$. The solution for t is $t = \log(\$4{,}300/\$4{,}000)/\log(1.04) = 1.8439\ldots$ years.

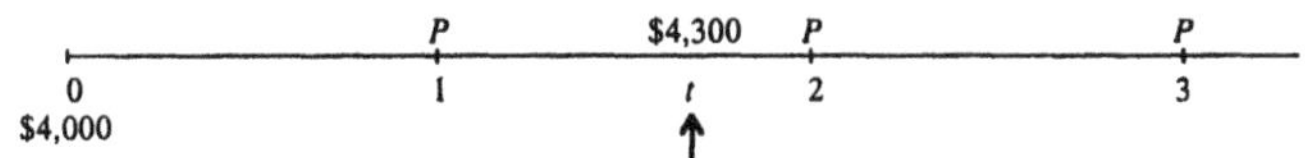

Time Diagram for Exercise 2.2.1

2.2.2 The interest rate per quarter is $i = .05/4 = .0125$. From the time diagram below we can write the equation of value $\$50(1.0125)^3 + \$75(1.0125)^2 = \$60(1.0125) + P$. This gives $P = \$68.04$

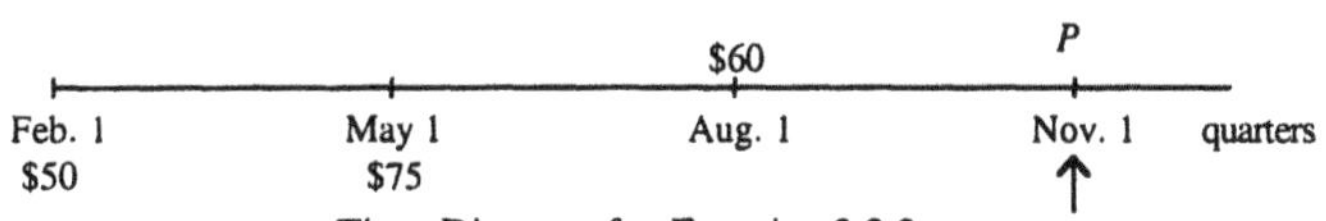

Time Diagram for Exercise 2.2.2

2.2.3 Looking at the time diagram below we write the equation of value $\$10{,}000 \doteq P(1.0615)^{-10} + P(1.0615)^{-11} + P(1.0615)^{-12} + P(1.0615)^{-13} + P(1.0615)^{-14} = P(2.4517479\ldots)$ so that $P = \$4{,}078.72$.

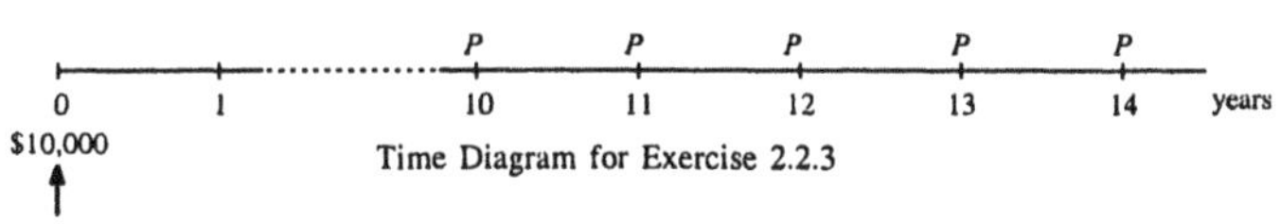

Time Diagram for Exercise 2.2.3

2.2.4 The interest rate per month is $i = .06/12 = .005$.

a) The amount of Stanley's loan is

$$L = \$3{,}000(1.005)^{-15} + \$3{,}000(1.005)^{-27} + \$3{,}000(1.005)^{-39} = \$7{,}875.48.$$

b) We need to find the time when a single payment of \$9,000 would be equivalent to the loan of \$7,875.48 which in turn is equivalent to the three equal payments of \$3,000. From the time diagram we write the equation of value

$\$7,875.48(1.005)^t = \$9,000$. The solution is $t = 26.761$ months.

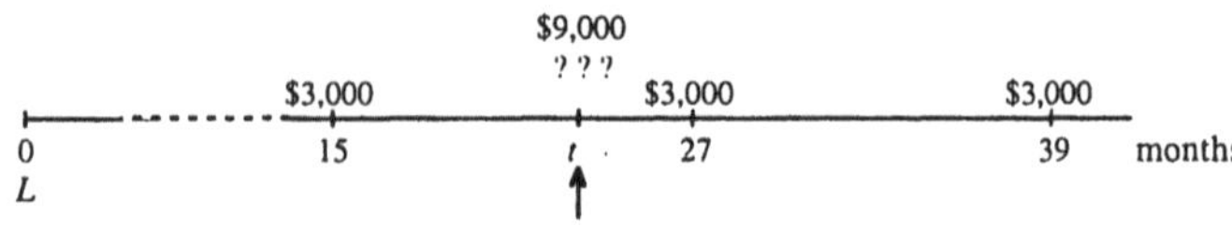

Time Diagram for Exercise 2.2.4

2.2.5 The period is the month and the interest rate per month is $i = .091/12 = .00758\overline{3}$. I put the focal date at time 0, but the solution would be unchanged wherever I put it. Using the time diagram as a guide we can write an equation of value. $\$10,000(1.00758\overline{3})^{12} + \$8,000(1.00758\overline{3})^{6} = P(1.00758\overline{3})^{-6} + P(1.00758\overline{3})^{-7} + P(1.00758\overline{3})^{-8} + P(1.00758\overline{3})^{-9} = P(3.77979\ldots)$ or $\$19,319.90 = P(3.77979\ldots)$ and finally, $P = \$5,111.36$.

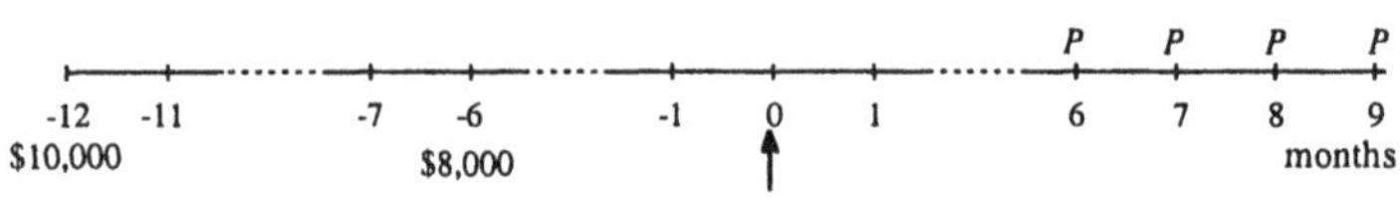

Time Diagram for Exercise 2.2.5

2.2.6 The period is the month and the monthly interest rate is $i = .0375/12 = 003125$. Below is a Time Diagram for Babe's saving strategy.

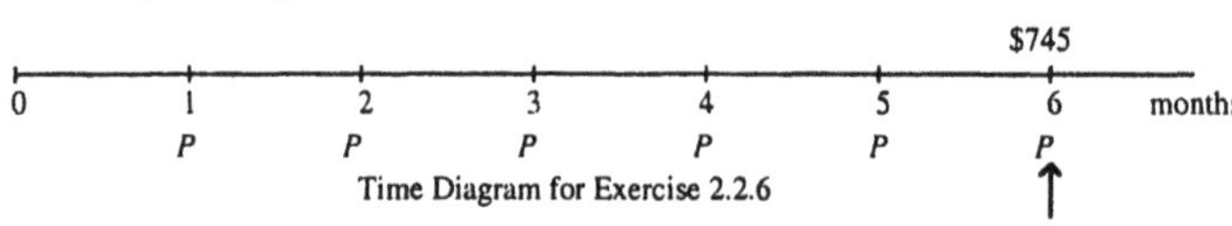

Time Diagram for Exercise 2.2.6

The equation of value with focal date at time 6 months is $\$745 = P(1.003125)^5 + P(1.003125)^4 + P(1.003125)^3 + P(1.003125)^2 + P(1.003125)^1 + P = P(6.047070\ldots)$ so $P = \$745/6.047070\ldots) = \$123.20$.

2.2.7 From the Time Diagram below we can write the equation of value

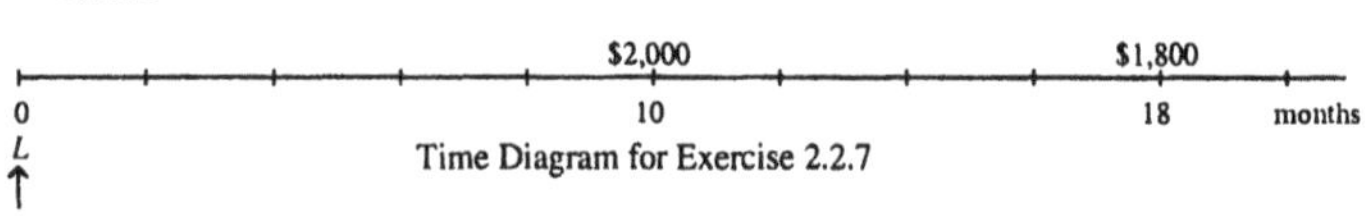

Time Diagram for Exercise 2.2.7

$$L = \$2,000(1.004\overline{3})^{-10} + \$1,800(1.004\overline{3})^{-18} = \$3,580.58.$$

2.2.8 Two and one-half years is 10 quarters, so two and one-half years earlier \$10,000 is worth $\$10{,}000(1.015)^{-10} = \$8{,}616.67$.

Exercises 2.3

2.3.1 Here's a story to go along with the equation of value:

$$\$23{,}000 = \$7{,}177.45(1.095)^{-1} + \$7{,}177.45(1.095)^{-2} + \$7{,}177.45(1.095)^{-3} + \$7{,}177.45(1.095)^{-4}.$$

Gustavo borrowed \$23,000 at annual interest rate 9.5% to make bail. He will repay the loan with 4 annual payments of \$7,177.45.

2.3.2 The equation of value in Formula 2.1 is

$$D_1(1+i)^{d-u_1} + D_2(1+i)^{d-u_2} + \ldots + D_r(1+i)^{d-u_r} = W_1(1+i)^{d-v_1} + W_2(1+i)^{d-v_2} + \ldots + W_s(1+i)^{d-v_s}.$$

We can factor of $(1+i)^d$ from both sides as follows:

$$(1+i)^d \{ D_1(1+i)^{-u_1} + D_2(1+i)^{-u_2} + \ldots + D_r(1+i)^{-u_r} \} = (1+i)^d \{ W_1(1+i)^{-v_1} + W_2(1+i)^{-v_2} + \ldots + W_s(1+i)^{-v_s} \}.$$

These common factors can then be cancelled to give

$$\{ D_1(1+i)^{-u_1} + D_2(1+i)^{-u_2} + \ldots + D_r(1+i)^{-u_r} \} = \{ W_1(1+i)^{-v_1} + W_2(1+i)^{-v_2} + \ldots + W_s(1+i)^{-v_s} \}.$$

2.3.3 The period is the month and the interest rate per month is $i = .09/12 = .0075$. There are three arrows in the time diagram-- one for each of parts a), b), and c). The equations of value with focal dates at times 0, 6 and 12 months are:

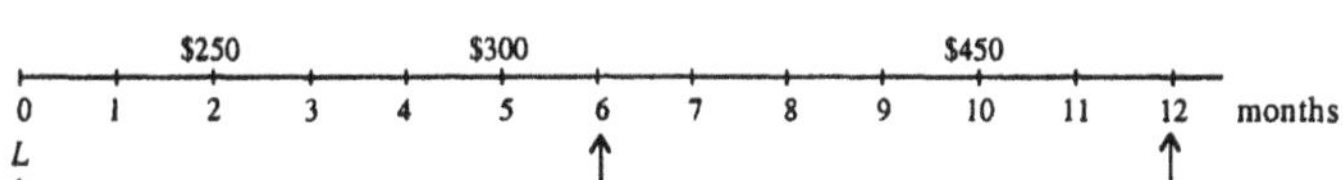

Time Diagram for Exercise 2.3.3

a) $L = \$250(1.0075)^{-2} + \$300(1.0075)^{-5} + \$450(1.0075)^{-10}$;

b) $L(1.0075)^6 = \$250(1.0075)^4 + \$300(1.0075) + \$450(1.0075)^{-4}$; and

c) $L(1.0075)^{12} = \$250(1.0075)^{10} + \$300(1.0075)^7 +$

$\$450(1.0075)^2$.

In the first time diagram we solve for L directly: $L = \$952.89$. In the second we calculate $L(1.04585\ldots) = \$996.58417\ldots$ so that $L = \$952.89$. In the third equation we get $L(1.09380\ldots) = \$1{,}042.27978\ldots$ so $L = \$952.89$ as expected.

2.3.4 The monthly interest rate is $i = .06/12 = .005$, so we can write $P = \$600(1.005) + \$800(1.005)^{-1} = \$1{,}399.02$ for the equivalent payment in 7 months.

2.3.5 In the time diagram below, I have put the deposits under the time line, and the withdrawals, including the final withdrawal, P, above the time line. I have also included the number of

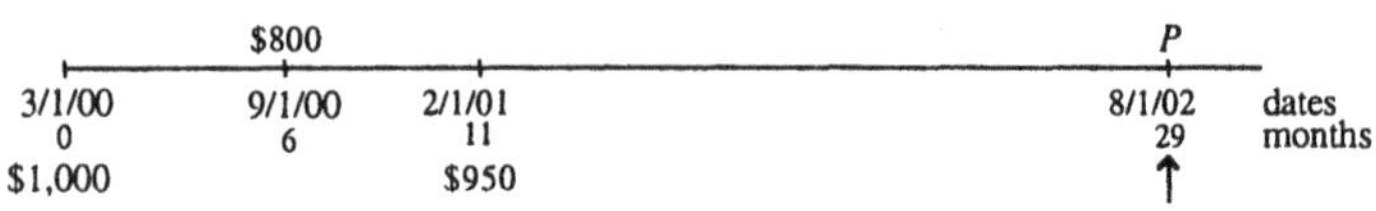

Time Diagram Illustrating Exercise 2.3.5

months measured from 3/1/00 under the time line. The equation of value sets the value of the deposits equal to the value of the withdrawals, all at 8/1/2002. With $i = j_{12}/12 = .051/12 = .00425$, we can write the equation of value

$$\$1{,}000(1.00425)^{29} + \$950(1.00425)^{18} = \$800(1.00425)^{23} + P.$$

Solving this equation for P gives $P = \$1{,}274.27$.

2.3.6 Let L denote the amount of Siomak's loan. Then L is the sum of the discounted values of all of Siomak's payments with $i = .05/4 = .0125$. That is,

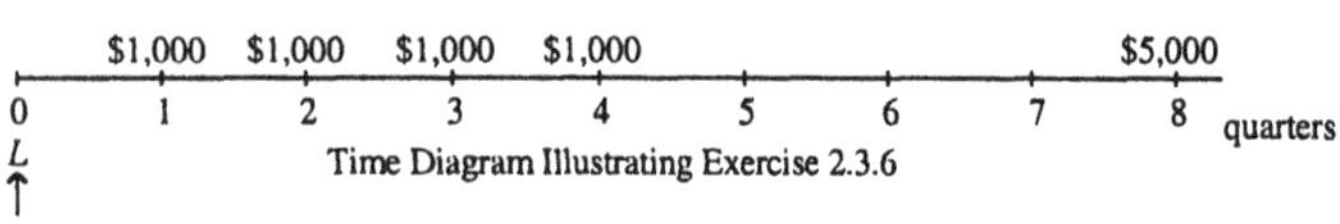

Time Diagram Illustrating Exercise 2.3.6

$$L = \$1{,}000(1.0125)^{-1} + \$1{,}000(1.0125)^{-2} + \$1{,}000(1.0125)^{-3}$$
$$+ \$1{,}000(1.0125)^{-4} + \$5000(1.0125)^{-8} = \$8{,}405.05.$$

Exercises 2.4

2.4.1 Steve's bank's nominal rate compounded semi-annually is (using Formula 2.3a)

$$j_2 = 2\left\{\left(1+\frac{.0475}{365}\right)^{365/2} - 1\right\} = 4.8065\ldots\%.$$

2.4.2 Lance's certificate is worth $\$5(1.0325)^{500}$ = \$44,055,503.45 in 1992.

2.4.3 We have the equation of value \$75,000$(1 + i)^2$ = \$76,000 which solved for i gives i = (\$76,000/\$75,000)$^{1/2}$ – 1 = .664...%.

2.4.4 We have the equation of value \$15,000 = \$6,900$(1 + i)^{-1}$ + \$6,900$(1 + i)^{-2}$ + \$6,900$(1 + i)^{-3}$. We'll set $h(i)$ = \$6,900$(1 + i)^{-1}$ + \$6,900$(1 + i)^{-2}$ + \$6,900$(1 + i)^{-3}$, the right-hand side of our equation of value and use Guess- and-Check to try to get $h(i)$ as close to \$15,000 as we can.

i	*h(i)*	*Comments*
.05	\$18,790.41	i = .05 is too low.
.10	\$17,159.28	
.15	\$15,754.25	
.20	\$14,534.72	Now we've passed the solution. We'll back up.
.175	\$15,123.47	Passed again.
.180	\$15,002.48	
.1805	\$14,990.48	.180 was closer.
.1801	\$15,000.08	We will stop here with four decimal places.

Harriet's loan is at the effective rate of 18.01%.

2.4.5 We have \$78,000 = \$21,000 + \$21,000$(1 + i)^{-1}$ + \$21,000$(1 + i)^{-2}$ + \$21,000$(1 + i)^{-3}$ for our equation of value. The value of i making the two sides equal is the effective rate. Set $m(i)$ = \$21,000 + \$21,000$(1 + i)^{-1}$ + \$21,000$(1 + i)^{-2}$ + \$21,000$(1 + i)^{-3}$. We will make a table and use Guess-and-Check to get close to the solution.

i	*m(i)*	*Comments*
.05	\$78,188.21	This is pretty close on the first guess.
.06	\$77,133.25	
.051	\$78,081.22	
.0515	\$78,027.85	.0515 is still too low, but close.
.0516	\$78,017.19	
.0517	\$78,006.52	
.05175	\$78,001.20	
.05176	\$78,000.13	This is now accurate to 5 decimal places

The effective rate is 5.176%.

2.4.6 Formula 2.2 gives the effective rate $j_1 = (1 + .0413/365)^{365} - 1 =$ 4.216...%.

2.4.7 Formula 2.3a gives $j_{12} = 12\{(1 + .0678/4)^{4/12} - 1\} = 6.742...\%$.

2.4.8 We write the equation of value

$$(1+i)^5 = \left(1+\frac{.04}{2}\right)^2\left(1+\frac{.06}{4}\right)^4\left(1+\frac{.08}{6}\right)^6\left(1+\frac{.10}{12}\right)^{24} = 1.4590745...$$

From $(1 + i)^5 = 1.4590745...$, we get $1 + i = (1.4590745...)^{1/5}$, and $i = (1.4590745...)^{1/5} - 1 = .0784884... = 7.84884...\%$.

2.4.9 From $\left(1+\frac{j_n}{n}\right)^n - 1 = \left(1+\frac{j_m}{m}\right)^m - 1$, we get $\left(1+\frac{j_n}{n}\right)^n = \left(1+\frac{j_m}{m}\right)^m$. Now we raise both sides to the power $1/n$ to get $1+\frac{j_n}{n} = \left(1+\frac{j_m}{m}\right)^{m/n}$, and $\frac{j_n}{n} = \left(1+\frac{j_m}{m}\right)^{m/n} - 1$, and this is Formula 2.3b. We get Formula 2.3a by multiplying both sides by n.

Miscellaneous Exercises – Chapter 2

2M1 The equation of value for this problem is $\$5,000(1.06)^n = \$6,000$. The solution is $n = \log(\$6,000/\$5,000)/\log(1.06) =$ 3.1290 years which is 3 years, 1 month and about 17 days.

2M2. The number of hairs on Seymour's head n years after Seymour was 30 is $985,912(1 - .14)^n = 985,912(.86)^n$. He will have 10,000 hairs left when $985,912(.86)^n = 10,000$. This happens in $n = \log(10,000/985,912)/\log(.86) = 30.44$ years after Seymour was 30 so Seymour will be about 60.

2M3. If Jörgen's investment tripled in 4 years, then the interest rate i satisfies the equation of value $(1 + i)^4 = 3$ so that $i = 3^{1/4} - 1 =$ .316074... His investment doubles in n years where n must satisfy $(1.316074...)^n = 2$. This happens in $n = \log(2)/\log(1.316074...) = 2.524$ years, or 2 years, 6 months and about 9 days.

2M4. We can write an equation of value with the help of the time diagram below:

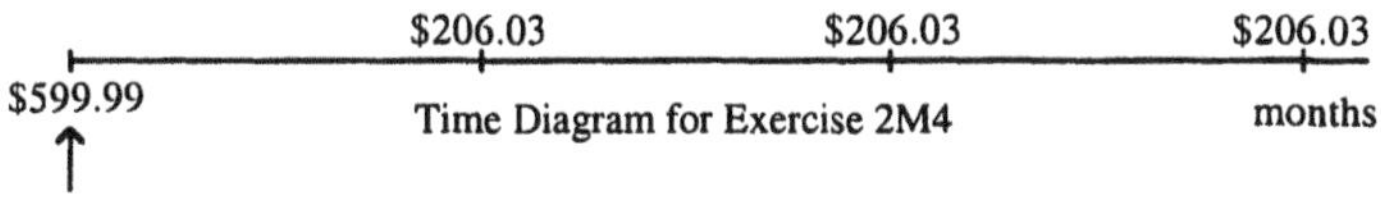

Time Diagram for Exercise 2M4

$\$599.99 = \$206.03(1+i)^{-1} + \$206.03(1+i)^{-2} + \$206.03(1+i)^{-3}$. We will use Guess-and-Check with i as the variable to make the right-hand side as close as we can to \$599.99. Set $c(i) = \$206.03(1+i)^{-1} + \$206.03(1+i)^{-2} + \$206.03(1+i)^{-3}$. Note that $i = j_{12}/12$. Here is a Guess-and-Check table:

i	$c(i)$	*Comments*
.05	\$561.07	.05 is too high.
.04	\$571.75	
.02	\$594.17	
.015	\$600.00	.015 is very close.
.0151	\$599.88	
.01501	\$599.99	This is correct to 5 decimal places.

a) The table shows that $j_{12}/12 = .01501$ so $j_{12} = .1801 =$ 18.01%.

b) The effective rate is $j_1 = (1 + j_{12}/12)^{12} - 1 \approx .19576 =$ 19.576%.

2M5. With the help of the time diagram below we can write the equation of value

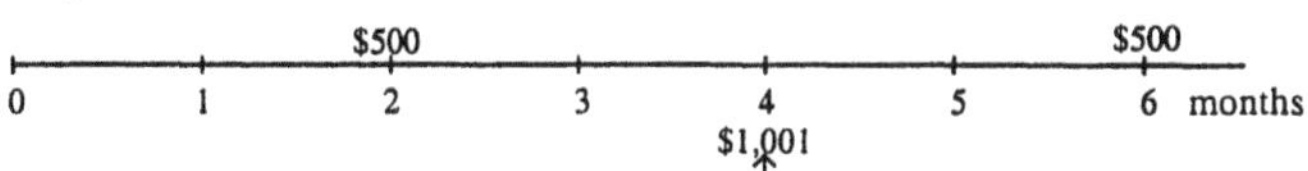

Time Diagram for Exercise 2.M.5.

$\$1{,}001 = \$500(1+i)^2 + \$500(1+i)^{-2}$, where $i = j_{12}/12$. Here is a Guess-and-Check table for $a(i) = \$500(1+i)^2 + \$500(1+i)^{-2}$.

i	$a(i)$	*Comments*
.05	\$1,004.76	
.04	\$1,003.08	
.02	\$1,000.78	Passed the solution.
.021	\$1,000.86	
.022	\$1,000.95	
.0225	\$1,000.99	We can get one more decimal place.
.0226	\$1,000.999	
.02261	\$1,000.9999	That's close enough.

We now have $j_{12}/12 = .02261$, so $j_{12} \approx .27132 = 27.132\%$.

2M6. Study the time diagram below:

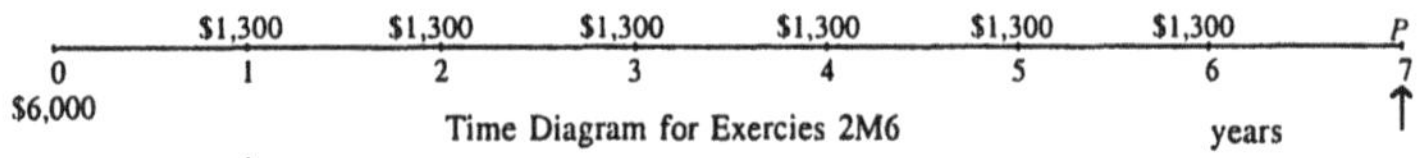

Time Diagram for Exercies 2M6

We need to evaluate all payments at the focal date of 7 years. The equation of value for this is

$$P + \$1,300\{(1.1)^6 + (1.1)^5 + (1.1)^4 +$$

$$(1.1)^3 + (1.1)^2 + (1.1)\} = \$6,000(1.1)^7.$$

We solve this for P to get $P = \$658.98$.

Chapter 3

Exercises 3.1

3.1.1 Here $a = 2{,}000(.9)^3$, $r = .9$ and $n = 75 - 2 = 73$, so the sum is

$$2{,}000(.9)^3 \frac{1-.9^{73}}{1-.9} = 14{,}573.3402073.$$

3.1.2 We can write $1 + 4 + 16 + 64 + ... + 1{,}048{,}576$ in the form

$$1 + 4 + 4^2 + 4^3 + \ldots + 4^{n-1}$$

where $4^{n-1} = 1{,}048{,}576$. From this we see that $a = 1$ and $r = 4$. Using the Log Rule or trial and error, we find $n - 1 = 10$ so that $n = 11$. The sum is

$$G_{11} = 1 \cdot \frac{4^{11}-1}{4-1} = 1{,}398{,}101.$$

3.1.3 The total paid is

$$G_{21} = \$30{,}000 + \$30{,}000(.8) + \$30{,}000(.8)^2 + \ldots$$

$$+ \$30{,}000(.8)^{20} = \$30{,}000\frac{1-.8^{21}}{1-.8} = \$148{,}616.49.$$

3.1.4 The monthly interest rate is $i = .084/12 = .007$. The equation of value is

$$\$2{,}400 = P(1.007)^{-1} + P(1.007)^{-2} + \ldots + P(1.007)^{-24}.$$

The right-hand side is a geometric sum with $a = P(1.007)^{-1}$, $r = (1.007)^{-1}$, and $n = 24$, so it sums to

$$P(1.007)^{-1}\frac{1-(1.007)^{-24}}{1-(1.007)^{-1}} = P(22.0216085\ldots),$$

so $\$2{,}400 = P(22.0216085\ldots)$, and $P = \$108.98$ is Ladislao's monthly payment.

3.1.5 The first alternative pays \$5,000,000. The second pays

$$G_{30} = \$.01 + \$.01(2) + \$.01(2^2) + \$.01(2^3) + \ldots$$

$$+ \$.01(2^{29}) = .01\frac{2^{30}-1}{2-1} = \$10{,}737{,}418.23,$$

so the second pays more than twice what the first does.

3.1.6 The thing to notice is that each term, except for a common factor of two, is a power of –2/9. The sum is therefore

$$G_{10} = 2 + 2(-2/9) + 2(-2/9)^2 + 2(-2/9)^3 + \ldots + 2(-2/9)^9.$$

The last exponent is 9 because there are 10 terms and the first one is $2(-2/9)^0$. We have $a = 2$, $r = -2/9$, and $n = 10$. The sum is

$$G_{10} = 2\frac{1-(-2/9)^{10}}{1-(-2/9)} = 1.63636315580.$$

3.1.7 The inputs for Formula 3.1 (a or b) are $a = (1.05)^2$, $r = 1.05$, and $n = 100$. The sum is therefore $G_{100} = 2{,}877.5527355\ldots$

3.1.8 Your parents make 2; your grandparents make 4 more; your great-grandparents make 8 more; ...; your great-great-great-great-great-great-great-great-great grandparents make 2,048 more for a total of $2 + 2^2 + 2^3 + \ldots + 2^{11} = 2\frac{2^{11}-1}{2-1} =$ 4,094. If you are not convinced, here is a table:

Ancestors	Number
Parents	2
Grandparents	$2^2 = 4$
Great-Grandparents	$2^3 = 8$
(Great)^2-grandparents	$2^4 = 16$
(Great)^3-grandparents	$2^5 = 32$
(Great)^4-grandparents	$2^6 = 64$
(Great)^5-grandparents	$2^7 = 128$
(Great)^6-grandparents	$2^8 = 256$
(Great)^7-grandparents	$2^9 = 512$
(Great)^8-grandparents	$2^{10} = 1{,}024$
(Great)^9-grandparents	$2^{11} = 2{,}048$

3.1.9 Balbino's payments may be written in the form of a geometric progression with $a = \$1{,}200$, $r = 1.06$, and $n = 10$. The sum of these terms is Balbino's accumulated value:

$$\$1{,}200\frac{(1.06)^{10}-1}{1.06-1} = \$15{,}816.95.$$

3.1.10 With the help of the time diagram below, we can write an equation of value using Equation 3.1a. We have \$13,040.16 as the sum, on one side of the

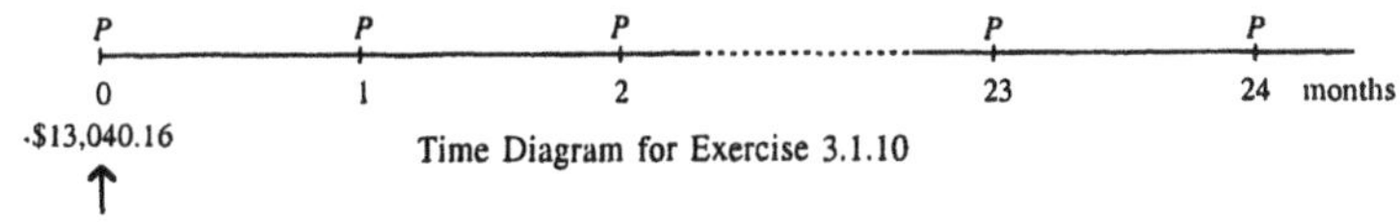

Time Diagram for Exercise 3.1.10

equation, and $P\dfrac{1-\left((1+\frac{.145}{12})^{-1}\right)^{25}}{1-(1+\frac{.145}{12})^{-1}}$ on the other. This is because we have $a = P$, $r = (1 + .145/12)^{-1}$, and $n = 25$ in Equation 3.1a. With a bit of work on our calculators, we get

$$\$13{,}040.16 = P\frac{1-\left((1+\frac{.145}{12})^{-1}\right)^{25}}{1-(1+\frac{.145}{12})^{-1}} = P(21.725634...),$$

so $P = \$13{,}040.16/21.725634... = \$600.22$.

3.1.11 Below is a time diagram for Simon's series of payments.

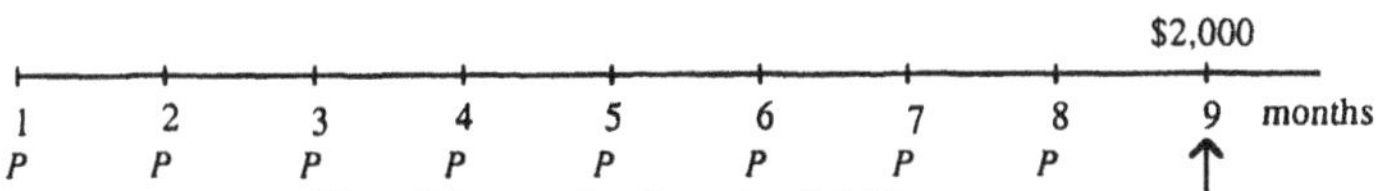

Time Diagram for Exercise 3.1.11

Let's write out the sum of the accumulated values of each payment. With monthly interest rate $i = .04/12 = .00\overline{3}$, we have

$$\$2{,}000 = P(1.00\overline{3})^8 + P(1.00\overline{3})^7 + ... + P(1.00\overline{3})^1.$$

Notice that we can look at the right-hand-side in two ways. First, as a geometric sum with $a = P(1.00\overline{3})^8$, $r = (1.00\overline{3})^{-1}$, and $n = 8$. On the other hand, we take the terms of the right-hand-side in reverse order, we could write $a = P(1.00\overline{3})^1$, $r = 1.00\overline{3}$, and $n = 8$. Using either Equation 3.1.a, or 3.1.b, the equation of value boils down to \$2,000 = $P(8.093958...)$, so $P = \$247.10$.

3.1.12 Given $G_n = a + ar + ar^2 + ar^3 + \dots + ar^{n-1}$ we multiply through r to get

$$rG_n = ar + ar^2 + ar^3 + \dots + ar^n.$$

Subtracting rG_n from G_n, and canceling like terms, we get

$$(1 - r)G_n = G_n - rG_n =$$

$$a + ar + ar^2 + ar^3 + \ldots + ar^{n-1} -$$

$$r(a + ar + ar^2 + ar^3 + \ldots + ar^{n-1}) =$$

$$a + ar + ar^2 + ar^3 + \ldots + ar^{n-1}$$

$$- \ (ar + ar^2 + ar^3 + \ldots + ar^{n-1} + ar^n)$$

$$a - ar^n = a(1 - r^n).$$

Now dividing both sides by $1 - r$, we have

$$G_n = a\frac{1 - r^n}{1 - r},$$

provided that $r \neq 1$. This is Formula 3.1 a. To obtain Formula 3.1b, multiply Equation 3.1a by (-1)/(-1).

Exercises 3.2

3.2.1 The equation of value is

$$S(P,\ 0.0734/12,\ 60,-1) = P\frac{1-(1.00611\overline{6})^{-60}}{0.00611\overline{6}} =$$

$$P(50.095171...) = \$17{,}345.40$$

which when solved for P gives $P = \$346.25$.

3.2.2 We have two annuities going in this problem. One is a 34-year annuity of P (to be determined) deposited monthly; the other is a 25-year annuity of \$2,141.09 payable monthly. The time diagram below shows you the layout

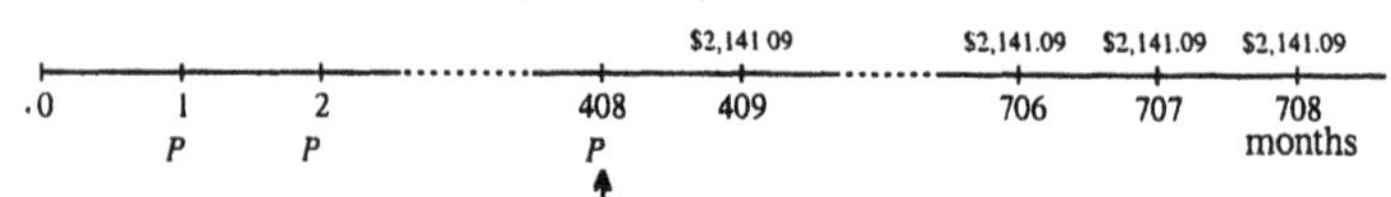

Time Diagram for Exercise 3.2.2

The number line runs from 0 to 408 (34×12) months for the first annuity and from 408 to 708 (25×12 = 300) months for the second annuity. The interest rate per month is $i = .082/12 = .0068\overline{3}$. The equation of value equates the values of each annuity at the arrow:

$$S(P,\ .0068\overline{3},\ 408,\ 407) = S(\$2{,}141.09,\ .0068\overline{3},\ 300,\ -1)$$

or

$$P\frac{(1.0068\overline{3})^{408}-1}{.0068\overline{3}} = \$2{,}141.09\frac{1-(1.0068\overline{3})^{-300}}{.0068\overline{3}}.$$

Notice that both sides are among the special cases of Formula 3.2. Solving for P yields $P = \$272{,}711.48/2{,}209.05 = \$123.45$.

3.2.3 The interest rate per month for Karen's loan is $i = j_{12}/12 = .0765/12 = .006375$ and the equation of value for the loan is

$$S(P,\ .006375,\ 60,\ -1) = P\frac{1-(1.006375)^{-60}}{.006375}$$
$$= P(49.72822...) = \$13{,}099.95$$

so $P = \$263.43$.

3.2.4 Using the time diagram below as a guide with the monthly

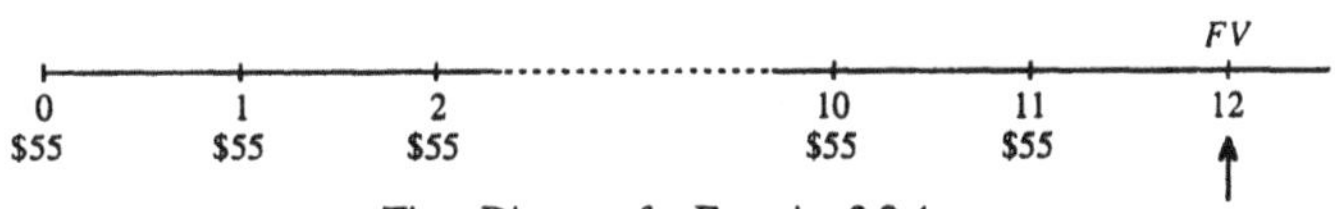

Time Diagram for Exercise 3.2.4

interest rate of $i = j_{12}/12 = .04/12 = .00\overline{3}$, the equation of value is

$$S(\$55,\ .00\overline{3},\ 12,\ 12) = \$55\frac{(1.00\overline{3})^{12}-1}{.00\overline{3}}(1.00\overline{3}) = \$674.48.$$

3.2.5 This is similar to Example 3.10. What Ron and M. J. owe is the accumulated value of their loan for eight years minus the accumulated value of the eight years of payments of \$1,002.52, all at $j_{12}/12 = .084/12 = .007$. They owe

$$\$125{,}550(1.007)^{96} - S(\$1{,}002.52,\ .007,\ 96,\ 95) =$$

$$\$125{,}550(1.007)^{96} - \$1{,}002.52\frac{(1.007)^{96}-1}{.007} =$$

$$\$108{,}703.13.$$

3.2.6 The monthly rate for this annuity is $i = .098/12 = .0081\overline{6}$ and its equation of value with focal date 45 years in the future is

$$S(P,.0081\overline{6},540,539) = P\frac{(1.0081\overline{6})^{540}-1}{.0081\overline{6}} = \$2{,}000{,}000.$$

Solving for P we get $P = \$204.65$.

3.2.7 Note that this problem is similar to Example 3.9. The period here is the quarter and the quarterly rate is $i = j_4/4 = .0742/4 = .01855$. The 30-years constitute 120 quarters, so Erik has 120 – 35 = 85 payments still to make. What he owes is the present value of these 85 payments of \$889.91:

$$S(\$889.91,\ .01855,\ 85,\ -1) = \$889.91\frac{1-(1.01855)^{-85}}{.01855}$$

$$= \$37{,}915.80.$$

3.2.8 This is something like the preceding problem except that it is n that we do not know. The monthly interest rate is $i = j_{12}/12 = .00625$. The equation of value is:

$$S(\$250,\ .00625,\ n,\ -1) = \$250\frac{1-(1.00625)^{-n}}{.00625} = \$27{,}049.30$$

and the solutions is $n = -\dfrac{\log\left(1-\frac{(\$27{,}049.30)(.00625)}{\$250}\right)}{\log(1.00625)} = 181.$

3.2.9 With the time diagram below as a guide and with the arrow at time 0 we can write the equation of value:

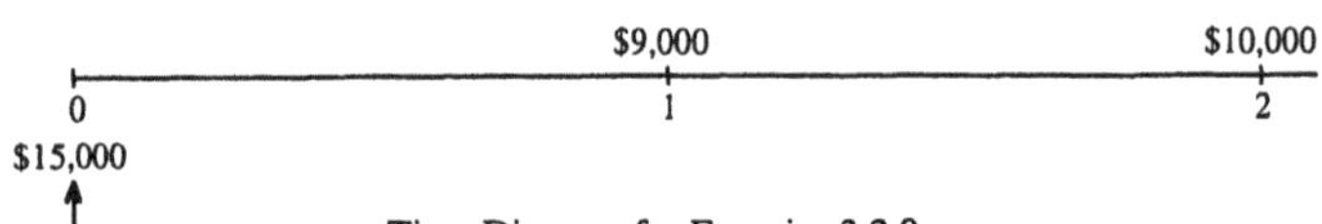

Time Diagram for Exercise 3.2.9

$\$15{,}000 = \$9{,}000(1+i)^{-1} + \$10{,}000(1+i)^{-2}$. We'll set

$$g(i) = \$9{,}000(1+i)^{-1} + \$10{,}000(1+i)^{-2}$$

and make a Guess-and-Check table to make $g(i)$ as close as we can to \$15,000.

i	*g(i)*	*Comments*
.05	\$17,641.72	.05 is too low.
.10	\$16,446.28	
.15	\$15,387.52	
.175	\$14,902.67	
.170	\$14,997.44	
.1699	\$14,999.35	Let's call it quits here.

Gene's yield rate was 16.99%.

3.2.10 The period is the month and the monthly interest rate is .075/12 = .00625. Study the time diagram below. We are looking for

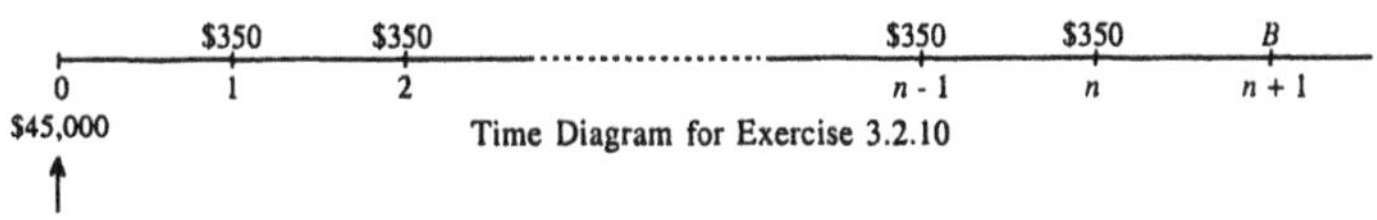

Time Diagram for Exercise 3.2.10

n, the number of equal payments and B, the final smaller payment. We will find n which must satisfy two conditions: it must be such that the present value of n payments of \$350 does not exceed \$45,000, but n +1 payments of \$350 does. The simplest thing to do is set the present value equal to \$45,000. The resulting n will almost certainly not be an integer, but the integer part of the number will be the correct value of n. So set

$$S(\$350,\ .00625,\ n,\ -1) = \$350\frac{1-(1.00625)^{-n}}{.00625} = \$45{,}000$$

and solve for n. The result is n = 261.2059... The means that 261 payments of \$350 does not pay off the loan, but 262 payments of \$350 is too much. As a check,

$$S(\$350,\ .00625,\ 261,\ -1) = \$44{,}985.88$$

and

$$S(\$350,\ .00625,\ 262,\ -1) = \$45{,}054.29.$$

But now with the help of our time diagram the equation of value is

$$S(\$350,\ .00625,\ 261,\ -1) + B(1.00625)^{-262}$$
$$= \$44{,}985.88 + B(1.00625)^{-262} = \$45{,}000$$

because adding the final payment will pay off the loan. Solving this for B we get B = (\$45,000 - \$44,985.88)$(1.00625)^{262}$ = \$72.25. So Sandy makes 261 equal payments of \$350 and a final payment of \$72.25 one month after the last payment of \$350.

3.2.11 This is similar to Example 3.11. The equation of value is

$$S(\$6,500,000,\ i,\ 20,\ 0) = \$6,500,000\frac{1-(1+i)^{-20}}{i}(1+i)$$

$$= \$49,290,168\,.$$

We'll set $J(i) = \$6,500,000\frac{1-(1+i)^{-20}}{i}(1+i)$ and make a Guess-and-Check table.

i	*J(i)*	*Comments*
.10	\$60,871,981	$i = .10$ is too low.
.15	\$46,788503	
.14	\$49,077,397	
.139	\$49,318,491	
.1391	\$49,294,277	
.13911	\$49,291,857	
.13912	\$49,289,437	This is right to 5 decimals

The interest rate assumed by the lottery commission is 13.912% annually.

3.2.12 The interest rate per month is .06/12 = .005 and the payments are at the beginning of every month for four years. The

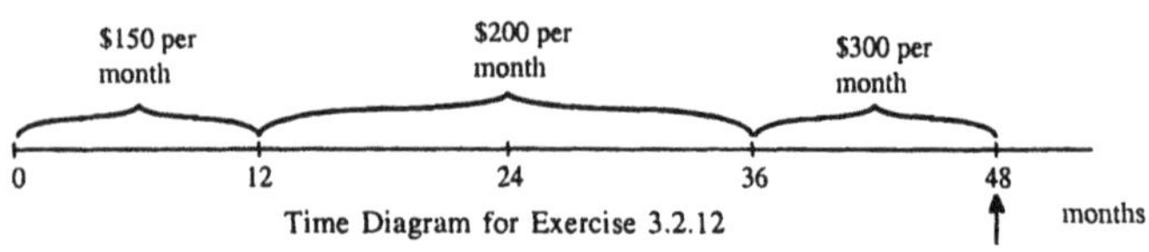

Time Diagram for Exercise 3.2.12

equation of value can be written as:

$$S(\$150,\ .005,\ 12,\ 48) + S(\$200,\ .005,\ 24,\ 36)$$

$$+S(\$300,\ .005,\ 12,\ 12) = \$2,225.33 + \$5,427.11 + \$3,719.17$$

$$= \$11,371.61.$$

3.2.13 With a monthly interest rate of i =.075/12 = .00625 for 240 = 20×12 months the price of Betsy's house was

$$S(\$744.39,\ .00625,\ 240,\ -1) = \$744.39\frac{1-(1.00625)^{-240}}{.00625}$$
$$= \$92{,}402.72.$$

3.2.14 Greg's monthly interest rate for 6×12 = 72 months is i = .0999/12 = .008325. The equation of value for his loan is:

$$S(P,\ .008325,\ 72,\ -1) = P\frac{1-(1.008325)^{-72}}{.008325} =$$
$$P(53.993361\ldots) = \$23{,}130.70$$

so $P = \$428.40$.

3.2.15 Neith's account has a monthly interest rate of $i = .004308\overline{3}$ and there are 14×12 = 168 deposits. The accumulated value of her account is:

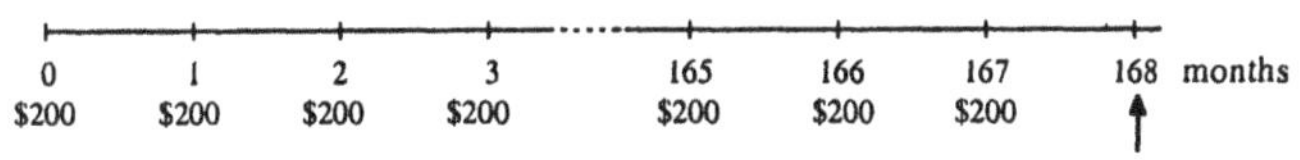

Time Diagram for Exercise 3.2.15

$$S(\$200,.004308\overline{3},168,168) =$$

$$\$200\frac{(1.004308\overline{3})^{168}-1}{.004308\overline{3}}(1.004308\overline{3}) = \$49{,}374.73.$$

3.2.16 The equation of value is:

$$S(\$1950,\ i,\ 12,\ -1) = \$1950\frac{1-(1+i)^{-12}}{i} = \$20{,}000$$

where $i = j_{12}/12$ is the monthly rate of interest. This is a Guess-and-Check problem. We'll set $h(i) = \$1950\frac{1-(1+i)^{-12}}{i}$ and make a table to get h as close to \$20,000 as we can.

i	*h(i)*	*Comments*
.05	\$17,283.34	.05 is too high.
.04	\$18,300.89	
.03	\$19,410.31	
.025	\$20,002.64	We will try to get closer.
.026	\$19,882.07	
.0251	\$19,990.54	
.02501	\$20,001.43	
.02502	\$20,000.22	We now have 5 decimal places.

Honest Slim is charging $j_{12} \approx 12(2.502) = 30.024\%$.

3.2.17 Remember our convention that when nothing is said about whether payments are being made at the end or the beginning of a period, the assumption is that are at the end. Dawson's deposits at the end of every month earn at the rate $i = .0575/12 = .004791\overline{6}$. In 5 years his deposits amount to \$15,000. The equation of value is:

Time Diagram for Exercise 3.2.17

$$S(P,\ .004791\overline{6},\ 60,\ 59) = P\frac{(1.004791\overline{6})^{60}-1}{.004791\overline{6}} =$$

$$P(69.323602\ldots) = \$15,000$$

so $P = \$216.38$.

3.2.18 Suzanne's payments are worth

$$S(\$645.74,\ .005,\ 90,\ -1) + \$1,250(1.005)^{-91} = \$47,501.17$$

to Beta Mortgage at $j_{12} = 6\%$.

3.2.19 The monthly interest rate Lloyd's money is earning is $i = .0445/12 = .003708\overline{3}$. His accumulated savings at the end of 14 years are:

$$S(\$150,\ .003708\overline{3},\ 84,\ 167) =$$

$$\$150\frac{1-(1.003708\overline{3})^{-84}}{.003708\overline{3}}(1.003708\overline{3})^{168} = \$20,130.90.$$

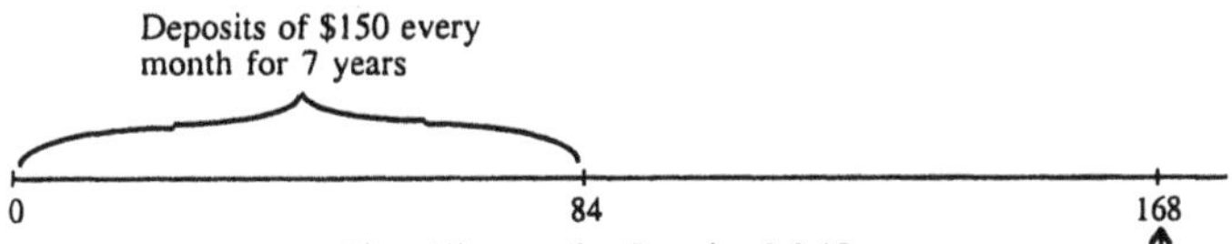

Time Diagram for Exercise 3.2.19

3.2.20 With interest per month at $i = .089/12 = .00741\overline{6}$ for $5 \times 12 = 60$ months Antonia can borrow

$$S(\$240,\ .00741\overline{6},\ 60,\ -1) = \$240\frac{1-(1.00741\overline{6})^{-60}}{.00741\overline{6}}$$

$= \$11{,}588.69$ for her car.

3.2.21 In the time diagram below, we have the focal date at time 0.

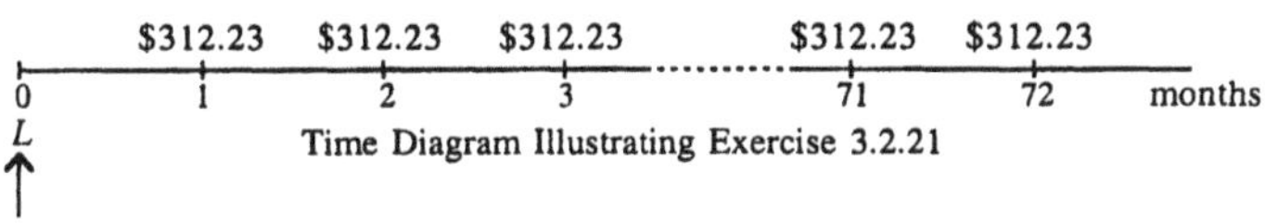

Time Diagram Illustrating Exercise 3.2.21

Using Formula 3.2a, the equation of value for this is

$$L = S(\$312.23,\ .0425/12,\ 72,\ -1) =$$

$$\$312.23\frac{1-(1.003541\overline{6})^{-72}}{.003541\overline{6}} = \$19{,}812.37.$$

3.2.22 Notice that I started the numbering in the time diagram below with 1. I could have run the numbers from 0 to 88 just as well. The point is to show you that the starting point does not matter

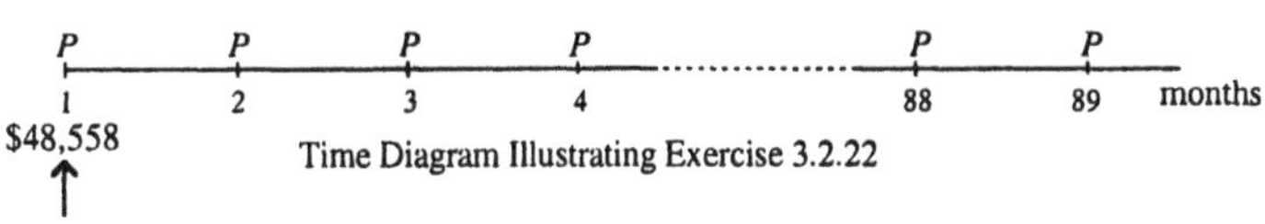

Time Diagram Illustrating Exercise 3.2.22

in calculating d. We just count from the arrow to the time of the first payment. In this case, we have $d = 0$. Using Formula 3.2b, the equation of value can be written

$$\$48{,}558 = S(P,\ .0712/12,\ 89,\ 0) =$$

$$P\frac{1-(1.0059\overline{3})^{-89}}{.0059\overline{3}}(1.0059\overline{3}) = P(69.3983779\ldots),$$

so that $P = \$48{,}558/69.3983779... = \$699.70$.

3.2.23 We want to know Luisa's balance at the end of 3 years = 12 quarters, so the arrow in the time diagram below is placed at the end of the three-year period.

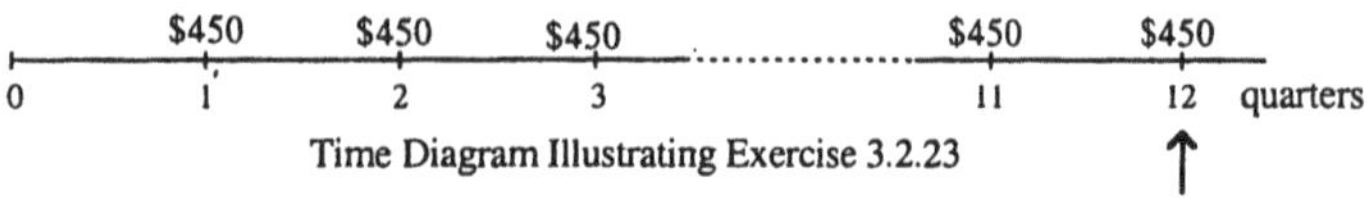

Time Diagram Illustrating Exercise 3.2.23

From Formula 3.2c, we write

$$S(\$450, .0614/4, 12, 11) = \$450\frac{(1.01535)^{12} - 1}{.01535} = \$5{,}880.15.$$

3.2.24 Tran makes 216 deposits of \$220, and we want the accumulated value of all the deposits one month after the last one. From Formula 3.2d, we write the accumulated value

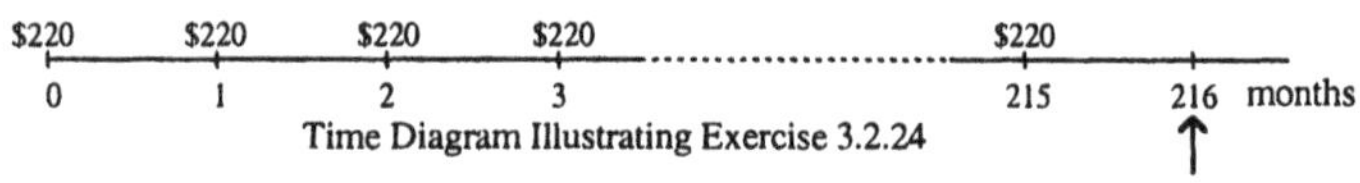

Time Diagram Illustrating Exercise 3.2.24

$$S(\$220, .07/12, 216, 216) = \$220\frac{(1.0058\overline{3})^{216} - 1}{.0058\overline{3}}(1.0058\overline{3})$$

$$= \$95{,}311.38.$$

3.2.25 We are looking for j_{12}, but first we will find $i = j_{12}/12$. Using Formula 3.2a,

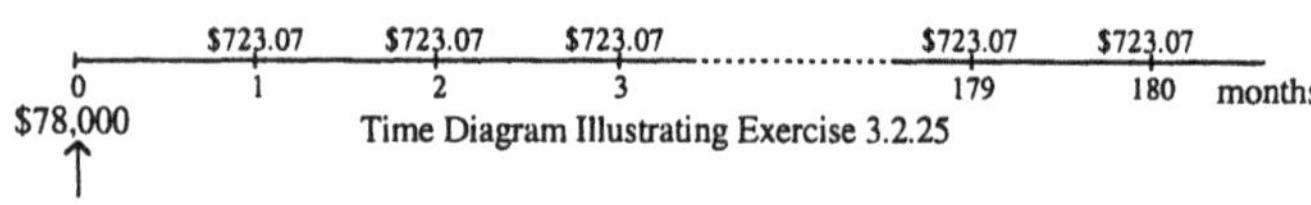

Time Diagram Illustrating Exercise 3.2.25

$$\$78{,}000 = S(\$723.07, i, 180, -1) = \$723.07\frac{1-(1+i)^{-180}}{i}.$$

Let $f(i) = \$723.07\frac{1-(1+i)^{-180}}{i}$. We will construct a Guess-and-Check table and try to find i so that $f(i) \approx \$78{,}000$.

i	$f(i)$	**Comments**
.02	$35,129.93	i = .02 is too high.
.01	$60,24740	i = .01 is much closer.
.0075	$72,289.94	We are still going in the right direction.
.006	$79,454.16	We are getting close.
.0061	$78,867.76	
.0062	$78,287.71	
.00625	$78,000.04	We can stop here

Guess-and-Check Table for Exercise 3.2.25

We have found $j_{12}/12 \approx .00625$, so $j_{12} \approx 12(.00625) = .075 = 7.5\%$.

Exercises 3.3

3.3.1 We want to know how fast Manolo's money is growing at time 10 years. Referring to Formula 3.4, set $Q(x) = \$10,000(1.06)^x$. Then the average rate of change of his money over the time-interval from 9.995 to 10.005 years is:

$$ROC(9.995, 10.005) = \frac{Q(10.005) - Q(9.995)}{10.005 - 9.995} =$$

$$\frac{\$10,000(1.06)^{10.005} - \$10,000(1.06)^{9.995}}{10.005 - 9.995} = \frac{10.4350741}{.01} =$$

$$\$1,043.51 \text{ per year.}$$

This approximates the rate at which Manolo's money is growing at 10 years.

3.3.2 The amount P that Keenan has to deposit now depends on the time it has been exposed to interest. We want to know how fast that amount is changing at time 15 years. We start with an equation of value:

$$P(1.06)^n = \$50,000$$

from which we get

$$P = \$50,000(1.06)^{-n} = Q(n).$$

We want to know how fast $Q(n)$ is changing when n = 15 years. We find:

$$ROC(14.999, 15.001) = \frac{Q(15.001) - Q(14.999)}{15.001 - 14.999} =$$

$$\frac{\$50{,}000(1.06)^{-15.001} - \$50{,}000(1.06)^{-14.999}}{15.001 - 14.999}$$

$$= -\$1{,}215.68 \text{ per year.}$$

The amount that Keenan needs to deposit now is decreasing at the rate of about $1,215.68 per year after 15 years.

3.3.3 The equation of value for Dr. Katz's loan is:

$$S(P,\ i,\ 15,\ -1) = P\frac{1-(1+i)^{-15}}{i} = \$228{,}500$$

which solved for P is:

$$P = \frac{\$228{,}500 \cdot i}{1-(1+i)^{-15}} = Q(i).$$

We want to know the rate at which this changes when $i = 9\%$. On the interval from 8.99% to 9.01% the average rate of change is:

$$ROC(8.99\%, 9.01\%) = \frac{Q(9.01\%) - Q(8.99\%)}{9.01\% - 8.99\%} =$$

$$\frac{\dfrac{\$228{,}500 \cdot .0901}{1-(1.0901)^{-15}} - \dfrac{\$228{,}500 \cdot .0899}{1-(1.0899)^{-15}}}{9.01\% - 8.99\%} = \$1{,}673.44$$

per 1% increase in the effective rate i.

3.3.4 a) If $i = .09$, Gilda can borrow:

$$S(\$6000,\ .09,\ 15,\ -1) = \$6{,}000\frac{1-(1.09)^{-15}}{.09} = \$48{,}364.13.$$

b) The amount that Gilda can borrow when the effective rate is i is:

$$S(\$6000,\ i,\ 15,\ -1) = \$6{,}000\frac{1-(1+i)^{-15}}{i} = Q(i)$$

and we want to know how fast this is decreasing when $i =$ 9%. The average rate of change on the interval from 9% to

9.01% is:

$$ROC(9\%,9.01\%) = \frac{Q(9.01\%) - Q(9\%)}{9.01\% - 9\%} =$$

$$\frac{\$6{,}000\dfrac{1-(1.0901)^{-15}}{.0901} - \$6{,}000\dfrac{1-(1.09)^{-15}}{.09}}{9.01\% - 9\%} =$$

$$= \text{-\$2,853.77}$$

per 1% increase in the effective rate.

3.3.5 We are looking for the rate of change of the height $H(t) = 6 + 30t - 16t^2$ when $t = 1.6$ seconds. If we take the interval from $t = 1.59$ seconds to 1.61 seconds, the average rate of change of the height of the ball is

$$\frac{H(1.61) - H(1.59)}{1.61 - 1.59} = \frac{12.8264 - 13.2504}{1.61 - 1.59}$$

$$= -21.2 \text{ feet per second.}$$

The ball is falling at the rate of 21.2 feet per second. Incidentally, we would get the same result no matter what interval centered at 1.6 that we took. In fact, 21.2 feet per second is the exact speed at which the ball is falling.

3.3.6 If $f(t) = at^2 + bt + c$, then

$$ROC(t-h, t+h) = \frac{f(t+h) - f(t-h)}{2h} =$$

$$\frac{a(t+h)^2 + b(t+h) + c - \{a(t-h)^2 + b(t-h) + c\}}{(t+h) - (t-h)} =$$

$$\frac{at^2 + 2ath + ah^2 + bt + bh + c - \{at^2 - 2ath + ah^2 + bt - bh + c\}}{2h} =$$

$$\frac{4ath + 2bh}{2h} = 2at + b.$$

This answer is free of h.

Miscellaneous Exercises – Chapter 3

3M1. The equation of value with focal date at time 0 is:

$$S(\$25{,}000,\ .066,\ 15,\ -10) = \$25{,}000\frac{1-(1.066)^{-15}}{.066}(1.066)^{-9}$$

$$= \$131{,}398.70.$$

3M2. This exercise is similar to Example 3.13 and Exercise 3.2.10. The period is the quarter and the interest rate per quarter is .0812/4 = .0203. Using the time diagram below, we write the equation of value:

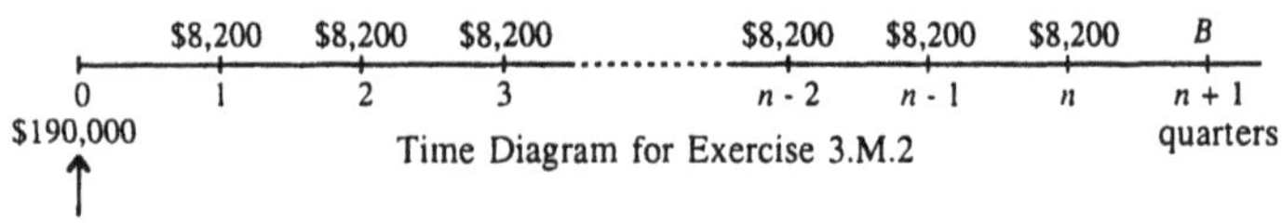

Time Diagram for Exercise 3.M.2

$$S(\$8200,\ .0203,\ n,\ -1) + B(1.0203)^{-(n+1)} =$$

$$\$8{,}200\frac{1-(1.0203)^{-n}}{.0203} + B(1.0203)^{-(n+1)} = \$190{,}000$$

where n is the number of quarters. We need to find n such that

$$\$8{,}200\frac{1-(1.0203)^{-n}}{.0203} < \$190{,}000,$$

but

$$\$8{,}200\frac{1-(1.0203)^{-(n+1)}}{.0203} > \$190{,}000.$$

The simplest way to do this is to find n such that $\$8{,}200\frac{1-(1.0203)^{-n}}{.0203} = 190{,}000$. Then the integer part of that number will be the correct n. Setting $\$8{,}200\frac{1-(1.0203)^{-n}}{.0203} =$ \$190,000 and solving for n we find n = 31.6255..., so the number of equal payments of \$8,200 is $n = 31$. In fact,

$$\$8{,}200\frac{1-(1.0203)^{-31}}{.0203} = \$187{,}293.56563106,$$

and

$$\$8,200\frac{1-(1.0203)^{-32}}{.0203} = \$191,604.00.$$

We can rewrite the equation of value now as:

$$S(\$8200,\ .0203,\ 31,\ -1)\ +\ B(1.0203)^{-32} =$$

$$\$8,200\frac{1-(1.0203)^{-31}}{.0203}\ +\ B(1.0203)^{-32} = \$190,000$$

or

$$\$187,293.56563106 + B(1.0203)^{-32} = \$190,000.$$

The solution is B = (\$190,000 - \$187,293.56563106)$(1.0203)^{32}$ = \$5,148.61.

3M3. If DeAnn were getting j_{12} = 7.9% or better, her monthly payments would be \$426.42 or less. This is the solution of the equation of value

$$S(P,\ .079/12,\ 60,\ -1) = \$21,080.14$$

for P. DeAnn is currently getting j_{12} = 8.1% as you could verify using Guess-and-Check.

3M4. From the time diagram below we can write the equation of value

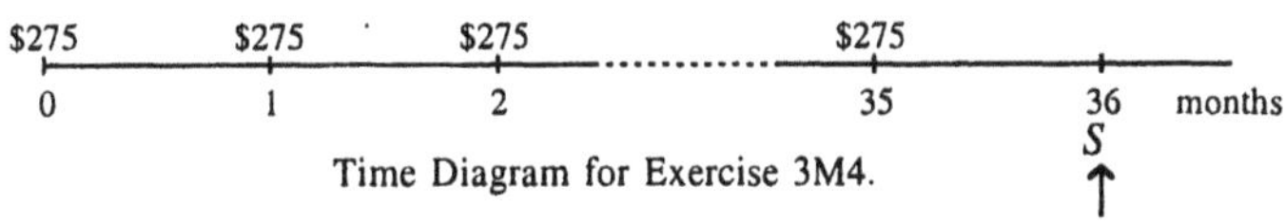

Time Diagram for Exercise 3M4.

$$S(\$275,\ .0515/12,\ 36,\ 36) =$$

$$\$275\frac{(1.004291\overline{6})^{36}-1}{.004291\overline{6}}(1.004291\overline{6}) = \$10,726.85.$$

3M5. In the time diagram below I have put the focal date at 11 months.

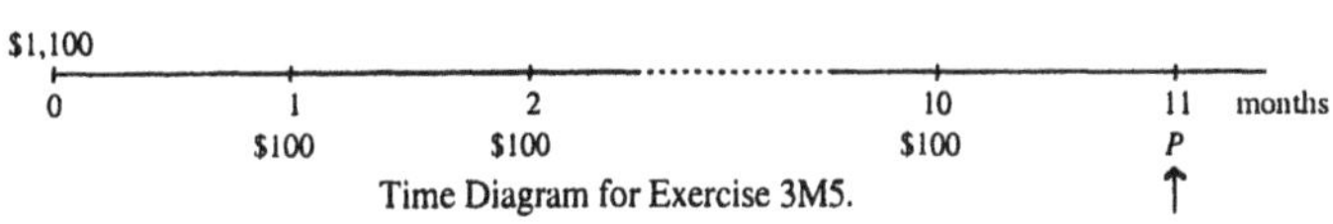

Time Diagram for Exercise 3M5.

Note that I could have put in anywhere and still gotten an equation of value equivalent to the one below:

$$\$1{,}100(1.00\overline{6})^{11} = S(\$100,\ .00\overline{6},\ 10,\ 10) + P.$$

We solve for P to get

$$P = \$1{,}100(1.00\overline{6})^{11} - S(\$100,\ .00\overline{6},\ 10,\ 10) = \$146.00.$$

Chapter 4

Exercises 4.1

4.1.1 We first need to find $j_{12}/12$ from j_{365}. The formula is

$$\frac{j_{12}}{12} = \left(1 + \frac{j_{365}}{365}\right)^{365/12} - 1 = \left(1 + \frac{.0475}{365}\right)^{365/12} - 1 = .00396591932.$$

After six years of monthly deposits, Maria's accumulated savings are:

$$S(\$150,\ .00396591943,\ 72,\ 71) = \$150\frac{(1.00396591943)^{72} - 1}{.00396591943} =$$

$$\$12{,}471.41.$$

4.1.2 We need the interest rate per month:

$$i = \frac{j_{12}}{12} = \left(1 + j_1\right)^{1/12} - 1 = (1.1)^{1/12} - 1 = .00797414043.$$

The equation of value for the loan is:

$$S(P,\ .00797414043,\ 60,\ -1) = P\frac{1 - (1.00797414043)^{-60}}{.00797414043}$$

$$= \$25{,}000.$$

Solving for P gives \$525.89.

4.1.3 We have the effective rate but need the monthly rate:

$$i = \frac{j_{12}}{12} = \left(1 + j_1\right)^{1/12} - 1 = (1.068)^{1/12} - 1 = .00549736708.$$

With the time diagram below as a guide we can write the equation of value:

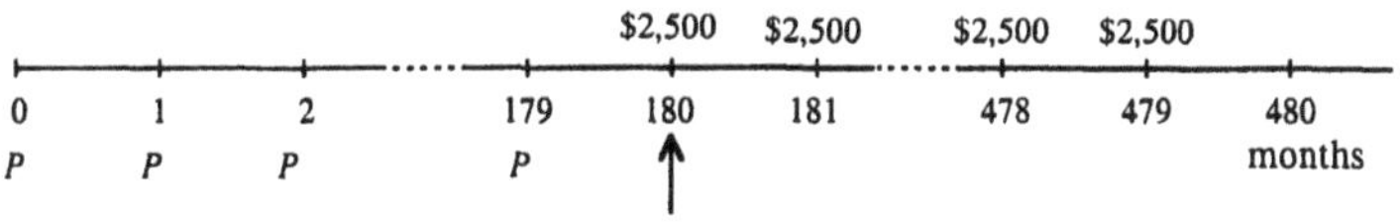

Time Diagram for Exercise 4.1.3

$$S(P,\ .00549736708,\ 180,\ 180) =$$

$$= S(\$2{,}500,\ .00549736708,\ 300,\ 0).$$

I have equated the two annuities at the focal date of 180. Let's write the equation out:

$$P\frac{(1.00549736708)^{180}-1}{.00549736708}(1.00549736708) =$$
$$\$2{,}500\frac{1-(1.00549736708)^{-300}}{.00549736708}(1.00549736708).$$

The solution is $P = \$1{,}198.87$.

4.1.4 We need the weekly interest rate. This is

$$i = \frac{j_{52}}{52} = \left(1+\frac{.054}{12}\right)^{12/52} - 1 = .00103666896.$$

Evelyn's savings after two years are $S(\$100,\ .00103666896,\ 104,\ 103) = \$10{,}975.33$.

4.1.5 The monthly interest rate is

$$i = \frac{j_{12}}{12} = (1+j_1)^{1/12} - 1 = (1.09)^{1/12} - 1 = .00720732332.$$

The equation of value is

$$S(P,\ .00720732332,\ 24,\ -1) = P\frac{1-(1.00720732332)^{-24}}{.00720732332} =$$

$$= P(21.966547\ldots) = \$3{,}300 - \$800 = \$2{,}500,$$

from which we get $P = \$2{,}500/21.966547\ldots = \$113.81$.

4.1.6 We are given $j_4 = 5\%$ but we need $i = j_{12}/12$. We have

$$i = \frac{j_{12}}{12} = \left(1+\frac{j_4}{4}\right)^{4/12} - 1 = (1.0125)^{1/3} - 1 = .00414942512.$$

Our equation of value is

$$S(P,.00414942512,60,59) = P\frac{(1.00414942512)^{60}-1}{.00414942512} =$$

$$P(67.9701972567) = \$25{,}000,$$

so $P = \$367.81$.

4.1.7 We'll need the monthly rate

$$i = \frac{j_{12}}{12} = \left(1 + j_1\right)^{1/12} - 1 = (1.086)^{1/12} - 1 = .00689878956.$$

Let P be the purchase price for the restaurant. Then

$$P - \$30{,}000 = S(\$1100, .00689878956, 96, -1) =$$

$$\$1{,}100\frac{1-(1.00689878956)^{-96}}{.00689878956} = \$77{,}038.02,$$

so Pablo paid P = \$77,038.02 + \$30,000 = \$107,038.02.

4.1.8 We need to convert the monthly interest rate to the equivalent effective rate. That's $j_1 = \{(1 + .072/12)^{12} - 1\}$ = 7.442416772%. Then, Madhu's accumulated savings at the end of 20 years are S(\$5,000, .07442416772, 20, 19) = \$215,156.86.

4.1.9 We need the monthly interest rate equivalent to the quarterly rate of 8%. That is, $i = j_{12}/12 = \{(1 + .08/4)^{4/12} - 1\}$ = .662270956%. Wai-Han's monthly payments P satisfy $S(P$, .00662270956, 360, 359) = \$385,000 - \$150,000. Solving for P gives us P = \$1,715.71.

4.1.10 We need the quarterly interest rate equivalent to the monthly rate of 7.5%. That is, $i = j_4/4 = \{(1 + .075/12)^{12/4} - 1\}$ = 1.886743164%. Yuri's quarterly deposits P satisfy $S(P$, .01886743164, 12, 11) = \$30,000. Solving for P gives us P = \$2,251.07.

Exercises 4.2

4.2.1 There are two annuities here. The contributions Tage and Berit make to their retirement fund and their increasing annuity. The inputs for the increasing annuity are P = 25,000 Crowns, i = .0725/12 = .006041666..., k = .0025, i^* = (.006041666...- .0025)/1.0025 = .00353293459, n = 300 and d = 0. With the help of the time diagram below, we can write the equation of value:

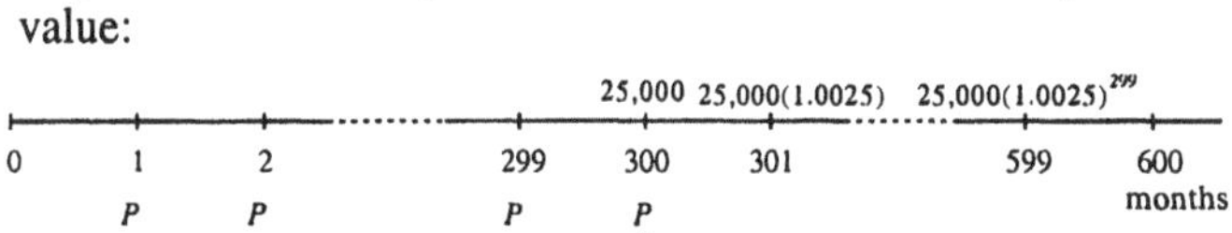

Time Diagram for Exercise 4.2,1

$$S(P,\ .006041\overline{6},\ 300,\ 299) = S^{(.0025)}(25000,\ .006041\overline{6},\ 300,\ 0).$$

Writing this out we get

$$P\frac{(1.006041\overline{6})^{300}-1}{.006041\overline{6}} =$$

$$25{,}000\frac{1-(1.00353283458)^{-300}}{.00353283458}(1.00353283458).$$

Carrying out the calculations and solving we get P = 5,500.35 Crowns.

4.2.2 For Formula 4.1 we have P to be determined, i = .005, k = .006, so that i^* = -.00099403579 (negative!), n = 360, and d = -1. Setting

$$\$750{,}000 = S^{(.006)}(P,\ .005,\ 360,\ \text{-}1) =$$

$$S(P,\ \text{-}.000994\ldots,\ 360,\ 0)(1.005)^{-1}$$

and solving for P yields P = \$1,742.12. The second payment is then \$1,742.12(1.006) = \$1,752.57 and the last is $\$1{,}742.12(1.006)^{359} = \$14{,}919.47$.

4.2.3 First look at the time diagram below to see the setup.

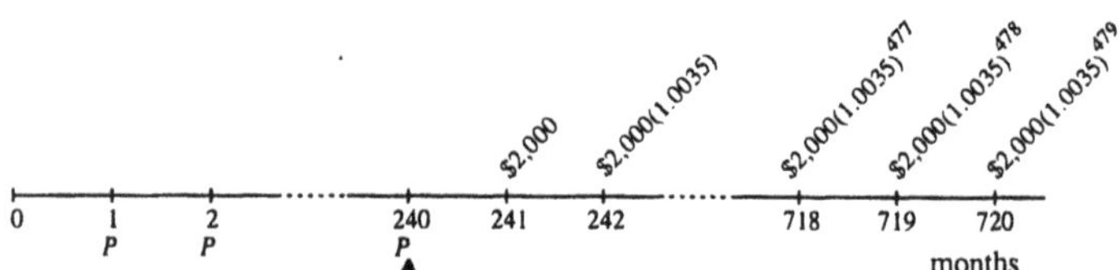

Time Diagram for Exercise 4.2.3

The annuity of P that Federico pays into his fund has the value

$$S(P,\ .0045,\ 240,\ 239) =$$

$$P\frac{(1.0045)^{240}-1}{.0045} = P(430.567557658),$$

at the focal date of 240 months, and this must equal the value of the increasing annuity at the same focal date. Noting that i^* = (.0045 - .0035)/1.0035 = .00099651221, that value is

$$S^{(.0035)}(\$2{,}000,\ .0045,\ 480,\ \text{-}1) =$$

$$S(\$2{,}000, .00099651221, 480, -1)(1.0035)^{-1}$$
$$= \$760{,}064.34.$$

Setting these two annuities equal and solving for P we get $P =$ \$1,765.26.

4.2.4 The monthly rate of interest is $i = .06/12 = .005$ and the equation of value is

$$S^{(k)}(\$600,\ .005,\ 72,\ 71) = \$600\frac{(1+i^*)^{72}-1}{i^*}(1+k)^{71} = \$60{,}000,$$

where $i^* = (.005 - k)/(1 + k)$. Substituting this expression into the equation of value and doing some rearranging we get

$$\$600\frac{(1.005)^{72}-(1+k)^{72}}{.005-k} = \$60{,}000,$$

and dividing by \$600, we get

$$\frac{(1.005)^{72}-(1+k)^{72}}{.005-k} = 100$$

Now set $M(k) = \dfrac{(1.005)^{72}-(1+k)^{72}}{.005-k}$. We'll make a Guess-and-Check table and try to get close to 100.

i	*M(i)*	***Comments***
.002	\$92.44	.002 is too low
.003	\$95.67	
.004	\$99.05	
.0045	\$100.80	Too high now.
.0044	\$100.44	
.0043	\$100.10	Let's try for two more places.
.00429	\$100.06	
.00428	\$100.03	
.00427	\$99.99	
.004271	\$99.997	
.004272	\$100.000	Can't get much closer.

Therefore, $k = .004272 = .4272\%$ is the percentage increase of Mool's deposits.

4.2.5 We begin with the sum, which we are calling $S^{(k)}(P, i, n, d)$,

$$P(1+i)^d + P(1+k)(1+i)^{d-1} + P(1+k)^2(1+i)^{d-2} + \ldots + P(1+k)^{n-1}(1+i)^{d-n+1}.$$

This is an n-term geometric sum with first term $a = P(1+i)^d$, and common ratio $r = (1+k)/(1+i)$. From Formula 3.1a, we have

$$S^{(k)}(P, i, n, d) = P(1+i)^d \frac{1-\left(\frac{1+k}{1+i}\right)^n}{1-\left(\frac{1+k}{1+i}\right)} =$$

$$P(1+i)^d \frac{1-\left(\frac{1+k}{1+i}\right)^n}{\frac{1+i}{1+i}-\frac{1+k}{1+i}} =$$

$$P(1+i)^d \frac{1-\left(\frac{1+k}{1+i}\right)^n}{\frac{i-k}{1+i}} = P\frac{1-\left(\frac{1+k}{1+i}\right)^n}{i-k}(1+i)^{d+1}.$$

4.2.6 We'll need $k = -.005$, $i = .087/12 = .00725$, $i^* = (.00725 + .005)/.995 = .01231155779$, and $d = 0$. The present value of Mario's insurance payments is

$$S^{(.005)}(\$24, .01231155779, 240, 0) =$$

$$\$24\frac{1-(1.01231155779)^{-240}}{.01231155779}(1.01231155779)$$

$$= \$1{,}868.72$$

4.2.7 We have $k = .0045$, $i = j_{12}/12 = .005$, $n = 120$, $i^* = .00049776008$, and $d = 119$.

a) Bibi Titi's last deposit will be $\$100(1.0045)^{119} = \$170.63$.

b) With the help of Formula 4.1, at the end of 10 years, Bibi Titi will have

$$S^{(.0045)}(\$100, .005, 120, 119) =$$

$$S(\$100,\ .00049776008,\ 120,\ 0)(1.005)^{119} = \$21{,}093.47.$$

c) We set \$21,093.47 = $S(P, .005, 120, 119)$ and find P = \$128.72.

4.2.8 We are given $i = .109/12 = .00908\overline{3}$, $k = .007$, so $i^* = .00206885137$, $n = 300$, and $d = -1$. To find the first payment P, set

$$S^{(.007)}(P,\ .00908\overline{3},\ 300,\ -1) =$$

$$S(P,\ .00206885137,\ 300,\ 0)(1.00908\overline{3})^{-1} =$$

\$125,000 and solve to find P = \$563.60. Zubeida's final payment will be $\$563.60(1.007)^{299} = \$4{,}537.11$.

4.2.9 The time diagram below tells most of the story. We calculate i^* from $i = .08/12 = .00\overline{6}$.

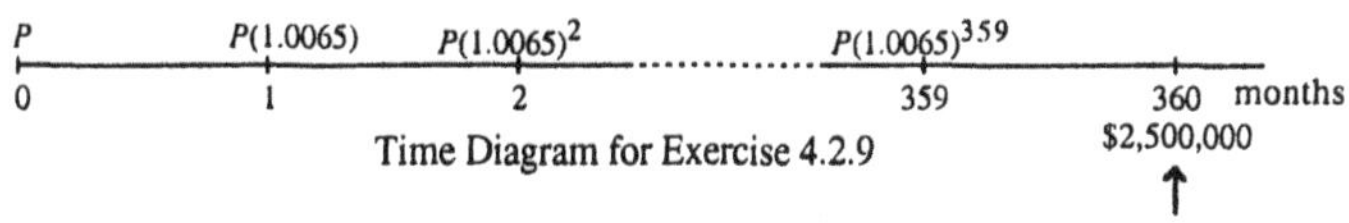

Time Diagram for Exercise 4.2.9

This gives $i^* = .00016559033$. We also have $n = 360$, and $d = 360$. We now set

$$S^{(.006)}(P,\ .00\overline{6},\ 360,\ 360) = \$2{,}500{,}000.$$

Solving for P gives us P = \$654.08. Dudley's last payment will be $\$654.08(1.0065)^{359} = \$6{,}695.45$

4.2.10 Here we set $S(P,\ .00\overline{6},\ 360,\ 360) = \$2{,}500{,}000$ and get P = \$1,666.34.

4.2.11 If $i = k$, $S^{(k)}(P, i, n, d)$ is the sum of a geometric progression with $a = P(1 + i)^d$, $r = 1$, and n terms. Since $r = 1$, all n terms are equal to the first, $P(1 + i)^d$. thus, Their sum is $nP(1 + i)^d$.

4.2.12 Here we have $k = .0035$ and $i = j_{12}/12 = .042/12 = .0035$, so $i = k$ and we may use the version for $S^{(k)}$ from Exercise 4.2.11. We have $S^{(k)}(P, i, n, d) = S^{(.0035)}(\$125, .0035\ 120,\ 119) = (120)(\$125)(1.0035)^{119} = \$22{,}733.12$.

Exercises 4.3

4.3.1 The inputs to Formula 3.2 for Bev's deposits are P = \$10,000, i = .08, n = 10, and d = 0. The inputs for Formula 4.3 for the perpetuity are P to be determined, i = .08 and $d = 0 - 10 = -10$. Using the time diagram below, we can write the equation of value:

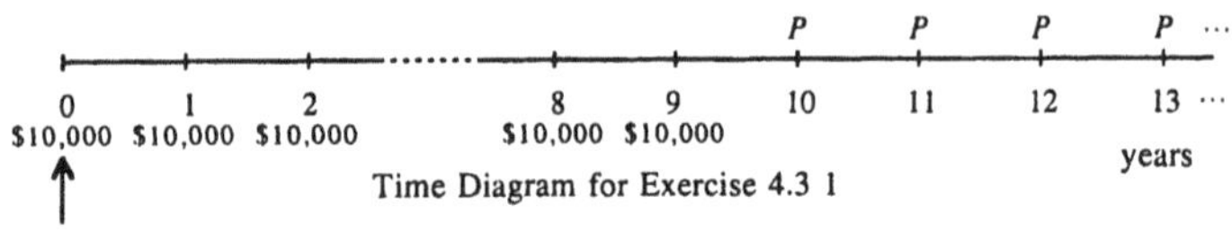

Time Diagram for Exercise 4.3 1

$$S(\$10000,\ .08,\ 10,\ 0) = S(P,\ .08,\ \infty,\ -10),$$

which, when written out becomes

$$\$10{,}000\frac{1-(1.08)^{-10}}{.08}(1.08) = P\frac{1.08^{-9}}{.08}.$$

Solving this for P yields P = \$11,589.25.

4.3.2 Using Formula 4.3, we see that Professor Ümläüt deposited

$$S(\$20000,\ .064,\ \infty,\ 0) = \$20{,}000\frac{1.064}{.064} = \$332{,}500.$$

4.3.3 Suzie's deposits amount to $S(\$30000,\ .086,\ 10,\ 10)$ = \$485,634.691356 at the end of 10 years. This money is to finance a perpetuity providing equal annual payments beginning at the end of the 10th year. Therefore

$$\$485{,}634.691356 = S(P,\ .086,\ \infty,\ 0) =$$

$$P\frac{1.086}{.086} = P(12.6279069767),$$

so P = \$38,457.26

4.3.4 We have \$176,891 = $\$9{,}413\frac{1+i}{i}$. This can be solved algebraically for i as follows:

$$\$9{,}413\frac{1+i}{i} = \$9{,}413\left(\frac{1}{i}+1\right),$$

so

$$\frac{1}{i}+1 = \$176{,}891/\$9{,}413 = 18.7922022735,$$

and

$$\frac{1}{i} = 17.7922022735,$$

and finally,

$$i = 1/17.7922022735 = .056204\ldots = 5.6204\ldots\%.$$

4.3.5 The present value of a perpetuity of \$8,000 at the end of every year at 10% effective is worth

$$S(\$8000, .10, \infty, -1) = \$8{,}000\frac{1}{.1}(1.1)^{0} = \$80{,}000.$$

4.3.6 First we must find the effective rate equivalent to $j_{12} = 12\%$. This is $j_1 = \{(1 + .12/12)^{12} - 1\} = 12.682503013\%$. The inputs for Formula 4.3 are $i = .12682503013$, $d = -4$, and P to be determined. We set

$$P\frac{(1.12682503013)^{-4+1}}{.12682503013} = \$150{,}000$$

and solve to get $P = \$27{,}218.59$.

4.3.7 In this problem we have an annuity and a perpetuity. Equating them at 20 years, we have

$$S(P, .09, \infty, 0) = P\frac{(1.09)^{0+1}}{.09} =$$

$$S(\$5000, .09, 20, 20) = \$5{,}000\frac{(1.09)^{20}-1}{.09}(1.09),$$

so $P = \$278{,}822.65/12.\overline{1} = \$23{,}022.05$

4.3.8 We will need to convert $j_2 = 10\%$ into the equivalent effective rate. This is $j_1 = \{(1 + .10/2)^2 - 1\} = .1025 = 10.25\%$. The present value of Vandana's perpetuity is

$$S(\$45000, .1025, \infty, -2) =$$

$$\$45{,}000\frac{(1.1025)^{-2+1}}{.1025} = \$398{,}208.06$$

4.3.9 We have $G = a + ar + ar^2 + ar^3 + \ldots$ If we multiply both sides of the equation by r, we get $rG = ar + ar^2 + ar^3 + \ldots$, and subtracting the latter from the former gives us $(1 - r)G = a$, all other terms canceling each other out. Dividing now by $1 - r$ gives Formula 4.2. Our derivation requires that $-1 < r < 1$.

Exercises 4.4

4.4.1 The present value of Bev's deposits is

$$S(\$10000,\ .08,\ 10,\ 0) =$$

$$\$10{,}000\frac{1-(1.08)^{-10}}{.08}(1.08) = \$72{,}468.88,$$

and using Formula 4.4b, we can write the present value of the increasing perpetuity as

$$S^{(.03)}(P,\ .08,\ \infty,\ -10) = P\frac{(1.08)^{-9}}{.08-.03}.$$

Setting the two equal and solving for P yields P = \$7,243.28 as the first scholarship award. The next two increase by 3% each and are \$7,460.58 and \$7,684.40.

4.4.2 We use Formula 4.4b for Jan-Ove's fund. The inputs are P = 100,000 Crowns,

$i = \left(1+\dfrac{.075}{12}\right)^{12} - 1 = .07763259886$, $k = .025$, and $d = 0$. Jan-Ove must provide

$$S^{(.025)}(100000,\ .077632\ldots,\ \infty,\ 0) = 100{,}000\frac{(1.077632\ldots)}{.077632\ldots-.025} =$$

2,047,462.26 Crowns.

4.4.3 If you use Formula 4.4a, Lois's single deposit looks like this:

$$S^{(.0325)}(\$120000,\ .078,\ \infty,\ 0) = \$120{,}000\frac{(1.04406779661)}{.04406779661}.$$

If you use Formula 4.4b the equation of value looks like this:

$$S^{(.0325)}(\$120000,\ .078,\ \infty,\ 0) = \$120{,}000\frac{(1.078)}{.078-.0325}.$$

In either case, the amount of the deposit is \$2,843,076.92.

4.4.4 From Formula 4.4b, we can write

$$\$2{,}500{,}000 = S^{(k)}(\$150000,\ .082,\ \infty,\ 0) = \$150{,}000\frac{(1.082)}{.082-k}.$$

This equation can be solved algebraically for k. After a little rearranging we get

$$.082 - k = .06492,$$

so

$$k = .01708 = 1.708\%.$$

4.4.5 This is an increasing perpetuity with P = \$300, i = 5.3%, k = 3.5%, and d = -1. We find

$$S^{(.035)}(\$300,\ .053,\ \infty,\ -1) = \$300\frac{(1.053)^{-1+1}}{.053-.035} = \$16{,}666.78.$$

4.4.6 Inputs for Zubeida's perpetuity are P = \$85,000, i = .085, k = .05, and d = 0, so her outlay is

$$S^{(.05)}(\$85000,\ .085,\ \infty,\ 0) = \$85{,}000\frac{(1.085)^{0+1}}{.085-.05} = \$2{,}635{,}000.$$

4.4.7 This is similar to Exercise 4.3.5 except that the dividends increase annually. For a yield of 10%, the investor should invest

$$S^{(.03)}(\$8000,\ .10,\ \infty,\ -1) = \$8{,}000\frac{(1.1)^{-1+1}}{.1-.03} = \$114{,}285.71.$$

4.4.8 This is an increasing perpetuity with P to be determined, i = .11, k = .06, and d = 0. Set

$$P\frac{(1.11)^{0+1}}{.11-.06} = \$400{,}000,$$

and solve for P to get P = \$18,018.02.

Exercises 4.5

4.5.1 a) $P = S(\$50,\ .06,\ 20,\ -1) + \$1{,}000(1.06)^{-20} = \$885.30$

b) $P = S(\$60,\ .05,\ 30,\ -1) + \$1{,}000(1.05)^{-30} = \$1{,}153.72$

c) $P = S(\$50,\ .045,\ 40,\ -1) + \$1{,}100(1.045)^{-40} = \$1{,}109.20$

4.5.2 Substituting the information given into Formula 4.5a, we have

$$\$5{,}814.90 = S(\$300, .05, 30, -1) + C(1.05)^{-30} =$$

$$\$300\frac{1-(1.05)^{-30}}{.05} + C(1.05)^{-30},$$

which has the solution $C \doteq \$5200.01$.

4.5.3 The inputs for using Formula 4.51 are P = \$10,980, F = \$10,000, r = .095/2 = .0475, n = 40, C = \$10,138.13. What we need to find is Rickie's annual yield rate j_2. We will begin by finding $i = j_2/2$. From Formula 4.41 we have

$$\$10{,}980 = S(\$475, i, 40, -1) + \$10{,}138.13(1 + i)^{-40} =$$

$$\$475\frac{1-(1+i)^{-40}}{i} + \$10{,}138.13(1+i)^{-40}.$$

We need to solve this by Guess-and-Check. Let

$$R(i) = \$475\frac{1-(1+i)^{-40}}{i} + \$10{,}138.13(1+i)^{-40}.$$

We will make a table and get as close as we can to \$10,980 as we can.

i	$R(i)$	Comments
.05	\$9,590.64	.05 is too high.
.04	\$11,513.23	.04 is too low.
.045	\$10,483.79	
.0425	\$10,980.00	Right on the nose.

Since $j_2/2 = .0425$, $j_2 = .085 = 8.5\%$.

4.5.4 For callable bonds with $i > r$, as we have here, the lowest price is at the latest possible date. We have i = .07, r = .055, $F = C$ = \$5,000 and n = 30 (the longest possible duration). Substituting these into Formula 4.5b, we calculate the price

$$P = S(-\$75, .07, 30, -1) + \$5{,}000 = \$4{,}069.32.$$

4.5.5 The inputs for Formula 4.5b are F = \$5,000, r = .03, C = \$5,250, i = .035, and n = 40. Bob's purchase price is

$$P = S(-\$33.75, .035, 40, -1) + \$5{,}250 = \$4{,}529.27.$$

4.5.6 This is equivalent to four \$25,000 bonds with coupons at j_2 = 8% redeemable at par; the first in 5 years, the second in 10 years, the third in 15 years, and the fourth in 20 years. The yield rate is j_2 = 6%. The purchase price for the serial bond is the sum of the prices of the individual bonds. These are:

$$P_1 = S(\$250, .03, 10, -1) + \$25{,}000 = \$27{,}132.55,$$

$$P_2 = S(\$250, .03, 20, -1) + \$25{,}000 = \$28{,}719.37,$$

$$P_3 = S(\$250, .03, 30, -1) + \$25{,}000 = \$29{,}900.11,$$

$$P_4 = S(\$250, .03, 40, -1) + \$25{,}000 = \$30{,}778.69,$$

and their sum is \$116,530.72.

4.5.7 We are given Formula 4.5a:

$$P = Fr\frac{1-(1+i)^{-n}}{i} + C(1+i)^{-n}.$$

This can be written successively as

$$P = Fr\frac{1-(1+i)^{-n}}{i} - \left(-C(1+i)^{-n}\right),$$

$$P = Fr\frac{1-(1+i)^{-n}}{i} - \left(C - C(1+i)^{-n} - C\right),$$

$$P = Fr\frac{1-(1+i)^{-n}}{i} - C\left(1-(1+i)^{-n}\right) + C,$$

$$P = Fr\frac{1-(1+i)^{-n}}{i} - Ci\frac{1-(1+i)^{-n}}{i} + C,$$

$$P = (Fr - Ci)\frac{1-(1+i)^{-n}}{i} + C.$$

This is Formula 4.5b.

4.5.8 The inputs for Formula 4.5a are $F = C = \$50{,}000$, $r = .06$, $i = .065$, and $n = 20$. The price of the bond is

$$P = S(\$3{,}000, .065, 20, -1) + \$50{,}000(1.065)^{-20} = \$47{,}245.37.$$

4.5.9 The only difference between this exercise and Exercise 4.5.5 is that here we are given the yield rate as an effective rate. To find Nadya's purchase price we will convert the yield rate of j_1

= 7% to the equivalent semiannual rate. When we do this we get $i = j_2/2 = \{(1 + .07)^{1/2} - 1\} = .03440804328$. Also, from Fr = \$150, Ci = \$180.64 we calculate the purchase price P = S(\$150 - \$180.64, .0344..., 40, -1) + \$5,250 = \$4,589.58.

Miscellaneous Exercises – Chapter 4

4M1. We can use Formula 3.2 with inputs P (to be determined), i = .08, n = 20, and d = 0:

$$S(P, .08, 20, 0) = P\frac{1-(1.08)^{-20}}{.08}(1.08) = P(10.6035992)$$

$$= \$2,650,899.80,$$

which gives P = \$250,000. Chauncey won the '\$5,000,000' lottery.

4M2. We are estimating the present value of an annuity increasing by 2.91262% annually. The inputs we need for Formula 4.1 are P = \$35,000, i = .06, k = .0291262, i^* = (.06 - .0291262)/1.0291262 = .03, n = 39, and d = -1. The estimated present value of loss of income is

$$S^{(.0291262)}(\$35,000, .06, 39, -1) =$$

$$S(\$35,000, .03, 39, 0)(1.06)^{-1} = \$775,694.33.$$

4M3. We need $i = \frac{j_4}{4} = \left(1+\frac{j_{12}}{12}\right)^{12/4} - 1 = .015075125$. Then the accumulated value of the 5-year annuity of \$300 per quarter is

$$S(\$300, .015075125, 20, 19) = \$300\frac{(1.015075125)^{20}-1}{.015075125}$$

$$= \$6,942.23.$$

4M4. The value of the cash option is the present value of Rosie's 20-year annuity of \$6,000,000 at j_1 = .06. That is

$$S(\$6,000,000, .06, 20, 0) = \$6,000,000\frac{1-(1.06)^{-20}}{.06}(1.06)$$

$$= \$72,948,698.95.$$

4M5. The details of this exercise are the same as they would be if Tomoko had bought a 5-year bond with $F = \$20{,}000$, $r = .05$, $i = .045$, $n = 10$, and C to be determined. Therefore, from

$$P = S(Fr, i, n, -1) + C(1 + i)^{-n},$$

we have

$$\$20{,}000 = S(\$1000, .045, 10, -1) + C(1.045)^{-10},$$

so

$$C = \{\$20{,}000 - S(\$1000, .045, 10, -1)\}(1.045)^{10}$$
$$= \$18{,}771.18.$$

Chapter 5

Exercises 5.2

5.2.1 To amortize a debt is to liquidate the debt by means of periodic payments.

5.2.2 a) From Formula 3.2 we have

$$S(P, .025, 20, -1) = P\frac{1-(1.025)^{-20}}{.025} = \$50{,}000,$$

so if Pavel could pay to the correct fraction of a penny, his payments would be $P = \$3{,}207.35643578$. Rounded up to the nearest dollar, Pavel will make his first 19 payments in the amount of $3,208.

b) If we let B denote Pavel's final payment, then it must satisfy the equation of value

$$S(\$3{,}208, .025, 19, -1) + B(1.025)^{-20} =$$

$$\$48{,}052.2834271 + B(1.025)^{-20} = \$50{,}000$$

The solution for B is $B = (\$50{,}000 - \$48{,}052.2834271)\cdot (1.025)^{20} = \$3{,}191.56$.

5.2.3 a) The amount Akira's monthly payments for the first 10 years is the solution of the equation of value

$$S(P, .105/12, 360, -1) = \$136{,}000.$$

That solution is $1,244.05.

b) We need to find what Akira owes on the original loan after 10 years of paying $1,244.05. We will use Formula 5.2 with inputs $P = \$1{,}244.05$, $i = .00875$, $n - r = 240$, and $d = -1$. Akira owes

$$S(\$1{,}244.05, .00875, 240, -1) = \$124{,}606.88.$$

If Akira now borrows this amount at $j_{12} = 7.2\%$ over the next 15 years, his payments will be the solution of the equation of value

$$S(P, .072/12, 180, -1) = \$124{,}606.88$$

for P. That solution is $P = \$1{,}133.98$.

5.2.4 This calls for Formula 3.2 with inputs P (to be determined), i = .06, n = 6, and d = –1. The equation of value is

$$\$16{,}000 = S(P, .06, 6, \text{-}1) =$$

$$P\frac{1-(1.06)^{-6}}{.06} = P(4.917324326)$$

and its solutions is P = \$3,253.80.

5.2.5 Here the period is the half-year and the interest rate per period is $i = j_2/\ 2 = .045$. Nadia's semi-annual payments must satisfy the equation

$$S(P, .045, 12, \text{-}1) = P\frac{1-(1.045)^{-12}}{.045} = \$16{,}000,$$

or P = \$1,754.66.

5.2.6 From the time diagram below we can write the equation of value

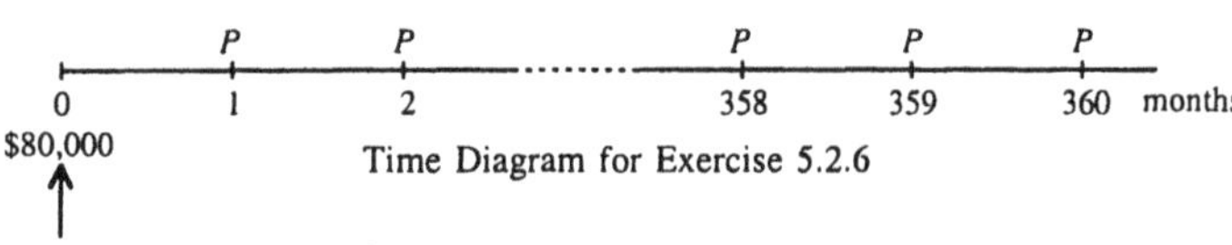

Time Diagram for Exercise 5.2.6

$$S(P, .09/12, 360, \text{-}1) = P\frac{1-(1.0075)^{-360}}{.0075} = \$80{,}000,$$

which gives the solution P = \$643.70.

5.2.7 The price of Michiko's house was S(\$715.12, .0799/12, 180, -1) = \$74,875.80.

5.2.8 The equation of value can be written

$$\$230{,}000 = S(\$1854.59, i, 240, \text{-}1) = \$1{,}854.59\frac{1-(1+i)^{-240}}{i},$$

which we can rewrite

$$\frac{1-(1+i)^{-240}}{i} = \$230{,}000/\$1{,}854.59 = 124.016629\ldots,$$

where $i = j_{12}/12$. Letting $M(i) = \dfrac{1-(1+i)^{-240}}{i}$, we will make a Guess-and-Check table trying to find i that gets $M(i)$ close to 124.016629...

i	$M(i)$	***Comments***
.01000	90.81942	$i = .01$ is too high.
.00500	139.58077	
.00600	127.00843	
.00650	121.35392	i will be between .006 and .0065
.00625	124.13213	
.00626	124.01915	This is close enough

Guess-and-Check Table for Exercise 5.2.8

We estimate $j_{12} = 12 \times .00626 = .07512 = 7.512\%$

5.2.9 We don't know the amount of the loan, nor do we know its term. But we have all we really need to find what Debra owes at the time she has 100 payments remaining. She owes the present value of 100 payments of \$1,248.13 at $j_{12} = 9.8\%$. Namely, Debra owes

$$S(\$1{,}248.13, .098/12, 100, -1) = \$85{,}070.97.$$

5.2.10 Using Formula 5.1, we find Carl-Axel's outstanding balance to be

$$\$15{,}559(1 + .07/12)^{32} - S(\$284.71, .07/12, 32, 31)$$

$$= \$8{,}757.30.$$

5.2.11 We can do this problem by the retrospective method using Formula 5.1 with $i = .12/12 = .01$. After his 70th payment, Sorie owes

$$\$30{,}000\,(1.01)^{70} - S(\$400, .01, 70, 69) =$$

$$\$30{,}000\,(1.01)^{70} - \$400\frac{(1.01)^{70}-1}{.01}$$

$$= \$19{,}932.37.$$

5.2.12 To use the prospective method, we need to know how many payments Nancy has remaining. The term of the loan, n, must satisfy the equation of value

$$S(\$826.15, .0734/12, n, -1) = \$826.15\frac{1-(1.00611\overline{6})^{-n}}{.00611\overline{6}}$$

$$= \$90{,}000.$$

The solution for n is $n = 179.999666514 \approx 180$. This discrepancy is going to cause a small disagreement between the two methods. With $n = 180$, we see that Nancy has $180 - 60 = 120$ payments of $826.15 left to make. Using Formula 5.2, we find her outstanding principal to be

$$OP_{120} = S(\$826.15, .00611\overline{6}, 120, -1) = \$70{,}090.92.$$

Now using Formula 5.1 to find Nancy's outstanding principal by the retrospective method, we have

$$OP_{120} = \$90{,}000(1.00611\overline{6})^{60} - S(\$826.15, .00611\overline{6}, 60, 59) =$$

$$\$129{,}760.68 - \$59{,}669.91 = \$70{,}090.77.$$

5.2.13 Andy's monthly payments are the solution of the equation of value

$$S(P, .088/12, 60, -1) = \$24{,}500$$

for P, the solution being $P = \$506.20$. After his 29th payment, Andy owes

$$S(\$506.20, .007\overline{3}, 31, -1) = \$13{,}990.70,$$

and the interest on that amount in the 30th payment is $(\$13{,}990.70)(.007\overline{3}) = \$102.60$.

5.2.14 Shira is to make 36 bi-monthly payments, so just after her 6th payment, she has 30 to go. We are going to need the amount of her payments. An equation of value for her loan is

$$S(P, .06/6, 36, -1) = P\frac{1-(1.01)^{-36}}{.01} = 60{,}000 \text{ shekels},$$

so $P = 1{,}992.86$ bi-monthly. Shira's outstanding principal just after her 6th payment is

$$S(\$1{,}992.86, .01, 30, -1) = 51{,}431.15 \text{ shekels}.$$

5.2.15 We are to show that

$$OP_r = L(1+i)^r - S(P,\ i,\ r,\ r-1) = S(P,\ i,\ n-r,\ -1),$$

where L, P, i, and n satisfy

$$L = S(P,\ i,\ n,\ -1) = P\frac{1-(1+i)^{-n}}{i}.$$

Substituting the right-hand side of the last equation into Formula 5.1, we get

$$OP_r = P\frac{1-(1+i)^{-n}}{i}(1+i)^r - P\frac{(1+i)^r - 1}{i} =$$

$$P\frac{(1+i)^r - (1+i)^{-(n-r)} - (1+i)^r + 1}{i} =$$

$$P\frac{1-(1+i)^{-(n-r)}}{i} = S(P,\ i,\ n-r,\ -1).$$

This last expression is the outstanding principal by Formula 5.2. Reversing the steps shows that the two are equivalent.

5.2.16 We are given enough information here to write the equation of value

$$\$62{,}819.38 = S(\$716.69,\ i,\ 132,\ -1),$$

where $i = j_{12}/12$ is what we are trying to find. The equation above can be rewritten

$$J(i) = \frac{1-(1+i)^{-132}}{i} = \$62{,}819.38/\$716.69 = 87.652095...$$

We will set up a Guess-and-Check table for this equation.

i	*J*(*i*)	***Comments***
.01000	73.11075	$i = .01$ is too low.
.00500	96.45960	
.00750	83.60642	
.00700	85.97030	
.00690	86.44473	
.00670	87.43556	
.00668	87.5345	
.00666	87.6337	This is close enough to stop.

Guess-and-Check Table for Exercise 5.2.16

We estimate j_{12} to be $12\times.00666 \approx .0799 = 7.99\%$

Exercises 5.3

5.3.1 Below is the amortization schedule for Norma's loan.

Year	*Annual Payment*	*Interest Paid*	*Principal Repaid*	*Outstanding Principal*
0	--	--	--	\$45,000.00
1	\$9,882.32	\$3,825.00	\$6,057.32	\$38,942.68
2	\$9,882.32	\$3,310.13	\$6,572.19	\$32,370.49
3	\$9,882.32	\$2,751.49	\$7,130.83	\$25,239.66
4	\$9,882.32	\$2,145.37	\$7,736.95	\$17,502.72
5	\$9,882.32	\$1,487.73	\$8,394.59	\$9,108.13
6	\$9,882.32	\$774.19	\$9,108.13	\$0.00

5.3.2 To find these quantities, we will need the amount of Merrick and April's monthly payment and the outstanding principal on their loan after their 74th payment. At that time they had 300 – 74 = 226 payments left to make. First, their monthly payment P satisfies

$$S(P, .071/12, 300, -1) = \$265{,}000,$$

and the solution is P = \$1,889.90. Next, their outstanding principal just after their 74th is

$$S(\$1{,}889.90,\ .00591\overline{6}, 226, -1) = \$235{,}212.59.$$

Therefore, the interest portion of their 75th payment is $\$235{,}212.59(.00591\overline{6}) = \$1{,}391.67$. The principal repaid is \$1,889.90 - \$1,391.67 = \$498.23.

5.3.3 Let OP_3 denote Sasha's outstanding principal after the third payment, let L denote the amount of his loan, and let P denote the amount of his payments. Then $(.12)L$ is the interest paid on his loan and therefore, the amount of his 4th payment must be $P = (.12)OP_3 + \$800$. On the other hand, P must satisfy

$$OP_3 = P\frac{1-(1.12)^{-5}}{.12} = P(3.60477620235).$$

Consequently, $P(3.60477620235) = (P - \$800)/.12 = 8.\overline{3}P - \$6,666.\overline{6}$, and so $P = \$1,409.87334656$. Finally,

$$L = S(P,\ .12,\ 8,\ -1) = P\frac{1-(1.12)^{-8}}{.12} = P(4.96763976684)$$

$$= \$7,003.74.$$

5.3.4 a) The amount of Kenito and Amy's monthly payments *P* are found from the equation of value

$$\$30,800 = S(P,\ .075/12,\ 240,\ -1)$$

to be $P = \$248.122703618$. From this we find their outstanding balance after their 11th payment to be $S(\$248.122703618, .00625, 229, -1) = \$30,168.6669295$. The interest paid in their next payment is therefore $(\$30,168.6669295)(.00625) = \$188.554168309$.

b) The amount of interest paid in the 12th payment can be written as

$$(.00625)\times S(\$248.122703618,\ .00625,\ 229,\ -1).$$

Similarly, the amount of interest paid in their 1st, 2nd , 3rd , ..., 11th payments can be written as

$$(.00625)\times S(\$248.122703618,\ .00625,\ 240,\ -1),$$

$$(.00625)\times S(\$248.122703618,\ .00625,\ 239,\ -1),$$

$$(.00625)\times S(\$248.122703618,\ .00625,\ 238,\ -1),\ \ldots$$

$$\ldots\ (.00625)\times S(\$248.122703618,\ .00625,\ 230,\ -1),$$

so that the total amount of interest paid in the first year is the sum of these 11 terms plus the one we already found on part a). We could evaluate each of these and add them up, but we can learn something for solving similar problems by writing everything out. The twelve interest payments can be written as follows:

$$\text{1st: } (.00625)\cdot\$248.12\ldots\cdot\frac{1-(1.00625)^{-240}}{.00625} =$$
$$\$248.12\ldots(1-(1.00625)^{-240)},$$

$$\text{2nd:}\$248.12\ldots(1-(1.00625)^{-239}),$$

3rd: $\$248.12\ldots(1 - (1.00625)^{-238})$,

. . .

11th: $\$248.12\ldots(1 - (1.00625)^{-230})$,

12th: $\$248.12\ldots(1 - (1.00625)^{-229})$,

When these are added, we get

$$\$248.12\ldots(12 - \{(1.00625)^{-229} + (1.00625)^{-230} + (1.00625)^{-239} + \ldots + (1.00625)^{-240})\}).$$

The term in braces is a geometric sum with

$$a = (1.00625)^{-229},\ r = (1.00625)^{-1},$$

and $n = 12$. The sum is \$2,286.57.

5.3.7 Jamila's interest rate per month is $i = j_{12}/12 = .084/12 = .007$. Her monthly payment is the solution for P of the equation of value

$$\$121{,}719.74 = S(P,\ .007,\ 360,\ -1) = P\frac{1-(1.007)^{-360}}{.007}$$

$$= P(131.26156061).$$

The solution is $P = \$927.31$.

a) After her 120th payment Jamila has 240 payments remaining. Her outstanding balance just after her 120th payment is $S(\$927.31, .007, 240, -1) = \$107{,}638.07$. We find this amount by using the payment value \$927.306817...internally. If we calculate with the rounded value of \$927.31, we get \$107,638.44 as Jamila's outstanding balance.

b) The interest on Jamila's 121st payment is $\$107{,}638.07 \cdot (.007) = \$753.47$. Therefore, the principal repaid is $\$927.31 - \$753.47 = \$173.84$.

5.3.8 We first find Raza's monthly payment. It is the solution for P in the equation of value

$$\$2{,}000 = S(P, .01, 6, -1) = P\frac{1-(1.01)^{-6}}{.01} = P(5.7954764746)$$

which yields P = \$345.096733421. In the table below, I will retain all possible decimal places internally, but display only two places:

Payment Number	***Payment Amount***	***Interest Paid***	***Principal Repaid***	***Outstanding Principal***
0				\$2,000.00
1	\$345.10	\$20.00	\$325.10	\$1,674.90
2	\$345.10	\$16.75	\$328.35	\$1,346.56
3	\$345.10	\$13.47	\$331.63	\$1,014.92
4	\$345.10	\$10.15	\$334.95	\$679.98
5	\$345.10	\$6.80	\$338.30	\$341.68
6	\$345.10	\$3.42	\$341.68	\$0.00

Amortization Schedule for Exercise 5.3.8

Exercises 5.4

5.4.1 We can solve this using formula 3.2 with inputs P (to be determined), i = .06, n = 15, d = 14. We are also given that $S(P, .06, 15, 14)$ = \$40,000. The solution P = \$1,718.51.

5.4.2 a) The annual interest payment is \$50,000(.11) = \$5,500.

b) The annual sinking fund deposit, P, must satisfy

$$S(P, .08, 10, 9) = \$50{,}000,$$

yielding P = \$3,451.47.

c) Total annual outlay is \$3,451.47 + \$5,500 = \$8,951.47.

d) If she amortized her loan at 11% annually, her annual outlay would be P', where P' satisfies $S(P', .11, 10, -1)$ = \$50,000. This value is P' = \$8,940.07.

5.4.3 Following Table 5.5, here is a sinking fund schedule:

Deposit Number	*Deposit Amount*	*Interest Earned in Fund at 8%*	*Increase in Fund*	*Amount Accumulated*
0	-	-	-	0.000
1	\$3,451.47	\$0.00	\$3,451.47	\$3,451.47
2	\$3,451.47	\$276.12	\$3,727.59	\$7,179.07
3	\$3,451.47	\$574.33	\$4,025.80	\$11,204.87
4	\$3,451.47	\$896.39	\$4,347.86	\$15,552.73
5	\$3,451.47	\$1,244.22	\$4,695.69	\$20,248.42
6	\$3,451.47	\$1,619.87	\$5,071.35	\$25,319.77
7	\$3,451.47	\$2,025.58	\$5,477.06	\$30,796.83
8	\$3,451.47	\$2,463.75	\$5,915.22	\$36,712.05
9	\$3,451.47	\$2,936.96	\$6,388.44	\$43,100.49
10	\$3,451.47	\$3,448.04	\$6,899.51	\$50,000.00

5.4.4 We can use Formula 3.2 with inputs $i = j_{12}/12 = .005$, $n = 15\times12 = 180$, and $d = 180 - 1 = 179$ to find P:

$$S(P, .005, 180, 179) = P\frac{1-(1.005)^{-180}}{.005} = \$100{,}000,$$

so $P = \$343.86$.

5.4.6 Koji's monthly payment P satisfies the equation of value

$$\$2{,}000 = S(P,\ .085/12,\ 6,\ 5) = P\frac{(1.00708\overline{3})^6 - 1}{.00708\overline{3}}$$

$$= P(6.10725881506),$$

so $P = \$327.479162184$. His interest payments are $(.10/12)\cdot(\$2{,}000) = \$16.67$. Below is a Sinking Fund Schedule showing the details.

Deposit Number	*Interest Payment*	*Deposit in Fund*	*Interest Earned in Fund at 8.5%*	*Increase in Fund*	*Amount Accumulated*
0					\$0.00
1	\$16.67	\$327.48	\$0.00	\$327.48	\$327.48
2	\$16.67	\$327.48	\$2.32	\$329.80	\$657.28
3	\$16.67	\$327.48	\$4.66	\$332.13	\$989.41
4	\$16.67	\$327.48	\$7.01	\$334.49	\$1,323.90
5	\$16.67	\$327.48	\$9.38	\$336.86	\$1,660.76
6	\$16.67	\$327.48	\$11.76	\$339.24	\$2,000.00

Sinking Fund Schedule for Exercise 5.4.6

5.4.7 We have the monthly rate $i = .0999885/12 = .008332375$. Nan is going to have to make n monthly payments, where

$$\$5{,}000 = S(\$293.43,\ .008332375,\ n,\ n-1) =$$

$$\$293.43\frac{(1.008332375)^n-1}{.008332375}.$$

The solution is $n = \log(1.14198232969)/\log(1.008332375) = 16$ months (almost exactly).

5.4.8 By amortization, STNX will pay P monthly, where P satisfies

$$\$2{,}200{,}000 = S(P,\ .0075,\ 120,\ -1)$$

$$= P\frac{1-(1.0075)^{-120}}{.0075} = P(78.9416926689),$$

so that P = \$27,868.67. On the other hand by the sinking fund method, STNX's monthly interest payments would be \$2,200,000(.095/12) = \$17,416.67, and their sinking fund deposits would be \$10,453.76 which is the solution for P' of the equation

$$\$2{,}200{,}000 = S(P',\ .1047/12,\ 120,\ 119).$$

The total outlay for the company by this method would be \$17,416.67 + \$10,453.76 = \$27,870.43, just \$1.76 more per month than by amortization.

Exercises 5.5

5.5.1 The equation of value for Gordy's transaction is

$$\$15{,}000 = \$900\frac{1-(1+i)^{-6}}{i} + \$16{,}500(1+i)^{-6}.$$

Here are a time diagram and Guess-and-Check table.

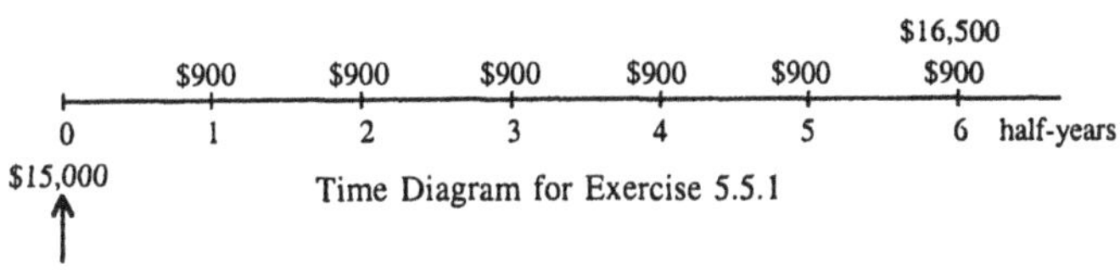

Time Diagram for Exercise 5.5.1

In the table,

$$G(i) = \$900\frac{1-(1+i)^{-6}}{i} + \$16{,}500(1+i)^{-6}.$$

i	$G(i)$	Comments
.05	\$16,880.68	.05 is too low.
.06	\$16,057.44	
.07	\$15,284.53	Getting close. Slow the descent.
.075	\$14,915.83	Too high now.
.074	\$14,988.65	Very close.
.0735	\$15,025.24	
.0736	\$15,017.91	
.0738	\$15,003.27	
.07385	\$14,999.62	
.07384	\$15,000.35	
.073845	\$14,999.98	This is a good place to stop.

What we have is $i = j_2/2 \approx .073845$, so Gordy's annual yield rate compounded semiannually is $j_2 \approx 14.77\%$.

5.5.2 Below is a time diagram for Rose's transaction.

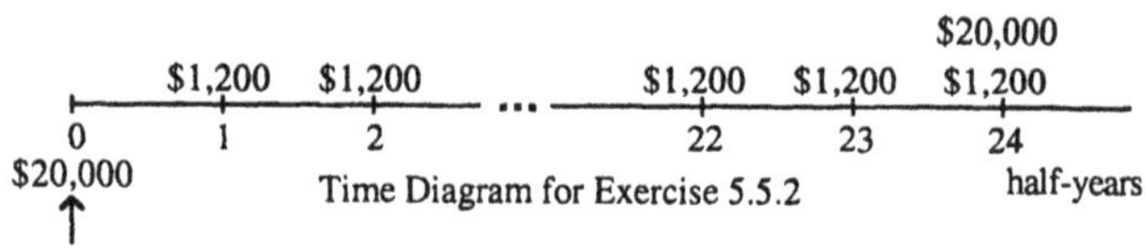

Time Diagram for Exercise 5.5.2

The equation of value for Rose' transaction is

$$\$20{,}000 = \$1{,}200\frac{1-(1+i)^{-24}}{i} + \$20{,}000(1+i)^{-24}$$

Although we could make a Guess-and-Check table, it is not necessary in this case. Because of the equality of the investment and its return, this particular problem can be solved algebraically. The equation of value can be rewritten as follows:

$$\$20{,}000\left(1-(1+i)^{-24}\right) = \$1{,}200\frac{1-(1+i)^{-24}}{i}.$$

Now cancel $\{1 - (1 + i)^{-24}\}$ from both sides and solve for i to get i = \$1,200/\$20,000 = .06. That is, i = .06 is the rate per half-year, so that the nominal annual yield compounded semi-annually is $j_2 = 12\%$.

5.5.3 Looking at the time diagram below, we can write the equation of value

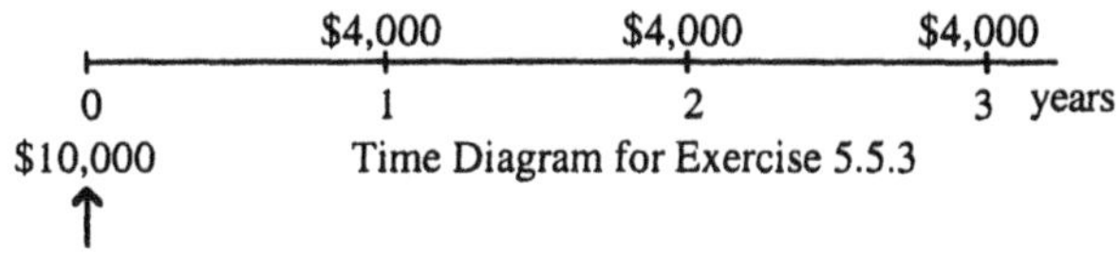

Time Diagram for Exercise 5.5.3

$$\$10{,}000 = S(\$4{,}000,\ i,\ 3,\ -1) = \$4{,}000\frac{1-(1+i)^{-3}}{i}.$$

We will make a Guess-and-Check Table to make $s(i) = \$4{,}000\frac{1-(1+i)^{-3}}{i}$ as close as we can to $10,000

i	*s(i)*	***Comments***
.05	$10,892.99	.05 is too low.
.06	$10,692.05	
.09	$10,125.18	
.095	$10,035.63	
.096	$10,017.88	
.097	$10,000.18	Good enough

Sandor's yield rate is around 9.7% annually.

5.5.4 To realize a yield rate of 10% Imre would have to pay P where P satisfies

$$\$10{,}000 = S(P,\ .10,\ 3,\ -1) =$$

$$P\frac{1-(1.1)^{-3}}{.1} = P(2.48685199098).$$

Thus, $P = \$4{,}021.15$.

5.5.5 The equation of value for this exercise is $\$5{,}000(1 + i)^4 = \$7{,}320.50$. The solution is $i = .10 = 10\%$. Damien's yield on his money was 10%.

5.5.6 A payment of $\$5{,}000(1.12)^4 = \$7{,}867.60$ would make Damien's yield rate 12%.

5.5.7 Let the yield rate per half-year be $i = j_2/2$. Then we can write the equation of value using Formula 4.5a:

$$\$9{,}850 = \$300\frac{1-(1+i)^{-20}}{i} + \$10{,}000(1 + i)^{-20}.$$

We will let $B(i) = \$300\frac{1-(1+i)^{-20}}{i} + \$10{,}000(1+i)^{-20}$ and use Guess-and-Check to find an i for which $B(i)$ is close to \$9,850.

i	*B(i)*	*Comments*
.05000	\$7,505.56	i = .05 is too high.
.04000	\$8,640.97	
.03000	\$10,000.00	
.03100	\$9,852.59	
.03101	\$9,851.13	One more tweak
.03102	\$9,849.67	This is good enough.

Guess-and-Check Table for Exercise 5.5.7

We estimate the nominal yield rate as $j_2 = 2(.03102) = 6.204\%$.

5.5.8 A purchase price of

$$P = S(\$300, .065/2, 20, -1) + \$10{,}000(1 + .065/2)^{-20} =$$

$$= \$9{,}636.52.$$

would yield $j_2 = 6.5\%$

Miscellaneous Exercises – Chapter 5

5M1. a)

Qtr.	*Interest Paid*	*Deposit in Fund*	*Interest Earned*	*Increase In Fund*	*Amount Accumulated*
0	--	--	--	--	\$0.00
1	\$80	\$977.78	\$0.00	\$977.78	\$977.78
2	\$80	\$977.78	\$14.67	\$992.45	\$1,970.22
3	\$80	\$977.78	\$29.55	\$1,007.33	\$2,977.56
4	\$80	\$977.78	\$44.66	\$1,022.44	\$4.000.00

b) Leah's total amount paid by the sinking fund method is 4×(\$80 + \$977.78) = \$4,231.12. By amortization at j_4 = 8%, she would pay P per quarter, where P satisfies

$$\$4{,}000 = P\frac{1-(1.02)^{-4}}{.02}.$$

The solution is P = \$1,050.50, so Leah's total outlay would be \$4,201.98.

5M2. Victor is going to need to make deposits of P into the sinking fund, where

$$\$10{,}000 = S(P, .025, 4, 3).$$

This yields P = \$2,408.18. The sinking fund schedule is

a)

Deposit No.	*Deposit*	*Interest Earned*	*Increase in Fund*	*Amount Accumulated*
0				\$0.00
1	\$2,408.18	\$0.00	\$2,408.18	\$2,408.18
2	\$2,408.18	\$60.20	\$2,468.38	\$4,876.56
3	\$2,408.18	\$121.91	\$2,530.09	\$7,406.65
4	\$2,408.18	\$185.17	\$2,593.35	\$10,000.00

b) By the above sinking fund method, Victor's total outlay is 4×(\$300 + \$2,408.18) = \$10,832.72. By amortization at j_2 = 6%, Victors semi-annual payments would be P = \$2,690.27 from the equation of value

$$\$10{,}000 = S(P, .03, 4, -1).$$

Victor's total outlay by amortization would therefore be 4×\$2,690.27 = \$10,761.08.

5M3. a) From the equation of value

$$\$28{,}000 = S(P, .0325, 16, 15),$$

we arrive at Joshua's semi-annual payments of P = \$1,361.92.

b) Joshua's semi-annual interest payments are .045×\$28,000 = \$1,260, so his total semi-annual outlay is \$1,361.92 + \$1,260 = \$2,621.92.

c) Had Joshua amortized the loan at 8% over 8 years, his semi-annual outlay would be the solution of the equation of value

$$\$28{,}000 = S(P, .045, 16, -1),$$

namely, P = \$2,492.43.

5M4. Tractor A's costs have a present value of

$$S(\$500, .06, 9, -1) + \$99{,}500 = \$102{,}900.85.$$

If Tractor B's price is P_B, then its total costs have a present value of

$$S(\$350, .06, 10, -1) + P_B,$$

and for this to equal the costs for Tractor A, Tractor B's price must be \$102,900.85 - S(\$350, .06, 10, -1) = \$102,900 - \$2,576.03 = \$100,324.82.

5M5. Michael's payments are the solution of the equation

$$S(P, .0725/12, 360, -1) = \$195{,}000,$$

giving P = \$1,330.24. Just after Michael's 120th payment,

$$\textit{Seller's Equity} = S(\$1{,}330.24, .0725/12, 240, -1)$$
$$= \$168{,}305.18,$$

$$\textit{Buyer's Equity} = \$195{,}000 - \textit{Seller's Equity} = \$26{,}694.82.$$

5M6. Per and Ulla's Balloon payment, B, is found from the equation of value

$$\$125{,}000 = S(\$925, .08/12, 299, -1) + B(1 + .08/12)^{-300},$$

which has the solution

$$B = \{\$125{,}000 - S(\$925, .08/12, 299, -1)\}(1 + .08/12)^{300}$$
$$= \$38{,}747.58.$$

5M7. We can use Formula 4.1 with inputs P (first payment to be determined), i = .072/12 = .006, n = 180, d = 180 – 1 = 179; i^* = .00399201597:

$$S^{(.002)}(P, .006, 180, 179) =$$

$$P\frac{1-(1.00399201597)^{-180}}{.00399201597}(1.00399201597)(1.006)^{179} =$$

$$P(127.96248532) = \$40{,}000,$$

from which we have P = \$106.50. The last payment is $P(1.002)^{179}$ = \$152.29.

5M8. Fredrik paid a fee of \$108,000(.03) = \$3,240 to the mortgage company. His monthly payments are P = \$819.303522814, which is the solution for P in the equation of value

$$\$108{,}000 = S(P, .078/12, 300, -1).$$

In effect, Fredrik has only borrowed \$108,000 - \$3,240 = \$104,760, but is paying \$819.303522814 per month for 25 years. His true interest rate $i = j_{12}/12$ per month satisfies the equation:

$$S(\$819.303522814, i, 300, -1) = \$104{,}760,$$

which can be rewritten as

$$F(i) = \frac{1-(1+i)^{-300}}{i} = 127.864701033.$$

Here is a Guess-and-Check table for this. I'll start with i = .078/12 = .0065.

i	$F(i)$	***Comments***
.006500	131.81928	i = .0065 is a little bit too low.
.007000	125.23492	We've passed i.
.006750	128.46001	
.006800	127.80447	
.006790	127.93515	
.006795	127.86978	That's pretty good

Guess-and-Check Table for Exercise 5M8.

We estimate j_{12} to be 12(.006795) = .08154 = 8.154%.

Chapter 6

Exercises 6.1

6.1.1 a) Yes; From property d), the probability is 1 - .31205 = .68795.

b) No. We do not have enough information to answer this.

6.1.2 The probability is 1 by property b).

6.1.3 Since the woman will either die between 70 and 90 or not, the probability of not dying in the interval is 1 – the probability of dying in the interval = 1 - .61313 = .38687 by property d).

6.1.4 No. Probabilities must be between 0 and 1 by property a).

6.1.5 The horse finishing both second and third is impossible, so the probability is 0 by property c).

6.1.6 The event 'at least one birthday match' is complementary to the event 'all have different birthdays,' so the probability is 1 - .2937 = .7063 by property d).

Exercises 6.2

6.2.1 The probability that a woman now aged 50 will die at age x is d_x/l_{50}, $x \geq 50$, so the age at which she is most likely to die is the age $x \geq 50$ where d_x is largest. A quick inspection of the table shows that this x is 85. The probability that (50) will die at 85 is d_{85}/l_{50} = 379,033/9,219,130 = .04111.

6.2.2 The probability that a 35-year-old woman will survive to age 70 and then die within the next two years is $(l_{70} - l_{72})/l_{35}$ = .03540 using Table II.

6.2.3 The probability that a 20-year-old male will die between the ages of 75 and 85 is $(l_{75} - l_{85})/l_{20}$ = .32360 using Table I.

6.2.4 See the Figure below.

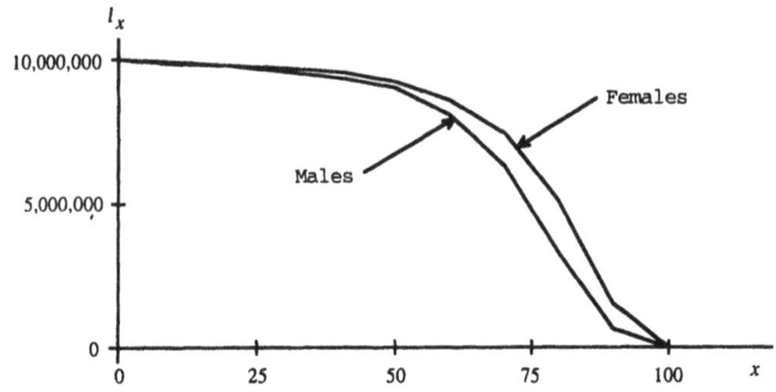

6.2.5 The man dies before age 64 with probability d_{63}/l_{63} = .02106, and survives to age 64 with probability 1 - .02106 = .97894. There is only a 2.106% chance that the insurance company will have to make a payment, so the man should pay \$100,000·(.02106) = \$2,106.

6.2.6. A 10-year-old boy dies at age 10 with probability d_{10}/l_{10} = .00073. A 51-year-old male dies at age 51 with probability 10(.00073) = .0073.

6.2.7. A 10-year-old girl dies at age 10 with probability d_{10}/l_{10} = .00068. A 54-year-old woman dies at age 54 with probability .00661, and a 55-year-old woman dies at that age with probability .00709. 10(.00068) = .0068 is about 40% of the way from .00661 to .00709, so the age we seek is about 54.4.

6.2.8. Using Table I, this is $(l_{70} - l_{80})/l_{28}$ = (6,274,160 - 3,274,541)/9,612,750 = .31205.

6.2.9. For males, we want ${}_{45}q_{35} = (l_{35} - l_{80})/l_{35}$ = (9,491,711 - 3,274,541)/9,491,711 = 0.65501

6.2.10. For females, we want ${}_{40}p_{40} = l_{40}/l_{40}$ = 5,056,025/9,545,345 = 0.52968.

6.2.11. For males, we want $(l_{60} - l_{70})/l_{20}$ = (8,084,266 - 6,274,160)/ 9,754,159 = 0.18557. I would expect the probability to be lower for females. 20-year-old females should be less likely to die as early as between 60 and 70 than males.

6.2.12. For females, we want $(l_{60} - l_{70})/l_{20}$ = (8,603,801 - 7,448,816)/9,820,821 = 0.11761. This *is* lower than the corresponding probability for males.

Exercises 6.3

6.3.1 Since ${}_{t|}q_{40} = d_{40+t}/l_{40}$, the sum equals $(d_{40} + d_{41} + ... + d_{99})/l_{40}$. Using Example 6.3, the last numerator is l_{40}, so that the last ratio is 1. In words, a 40-year-old is certain to die at one of the ages 40, 41, 42, ..., or 99.

6.3.2 ${}_{40|}q_0$ is the probability that a newborn will die at 40 whereas ${}_{0|}q_{40}$ is the probability that a 40-year-old will die at 40. For males,

$$ {}_{40|}q_0 = .00283 < .00302 = {}_{0|}q_{40}. $$

For females,

$$ {}_{40|}q_0 = .00231 < .00242 = {}_{0|}q_{40}. $$

6.3.3 a) The probability that (80) dies at age x is d_x/l_{80}, $x \geq 80$. d_x is highest when $x = 85$. Thus, age 85 is the most likely age at death for a woman aged 80.

b) The probability that (85) dies at age x is d_x/l_{85}, $x \geq 85$. d_x is highest when $x = 85$. Thus, age 85 is also the most likely age at death for a woman aged 85.

c) The two probabilities are not equal but they give the most likely ages at death for the two ages. The fact that a) and b) have the same answer owes to the fact that d_x peaks at $x = 85$.

6.3.4 A 40-year-old is not likely to die at any particular age, but 78 is the most likely of all ages. Since the probability of his dying at 78 is so low, you might rather say that 78 is his least unlikely age at death.

6.3.5 No. We know that ${}_{a|}q_x = \frac{d_{x+a}}{l_x}$ and ${}_{b|}q_x = \frac{d_{x+b}}{l_x}$. Just because we know that $a < b$ does not tell us which is the larger of ${}_{a|}q_x$ and ${}_{b|}q_x$. This is because the d_x columns of Tables I & II neither increase nor decrease steadily. They fluctuate.

6.3.6 The probability distribution of ages at death of 95-year-old women is composed of the numbers $\{{}_{0|}q_{95}, {}_{1|}q_{95}, {}_{2|}q_{95}, {}_{3|}q_{95}, {}_{4|}q_{95}\}$, where ${}_{t|}q_{95} = d_{95+t}/l_{95}$. From Table II, we find {0.31732, 0.25651, 0.20242, 0.14675, 0.07700}. Note that these five numbers sum to 1, as they should.

Exercises 6.4

6.4.1 From Table I for males, *AAD*(71) is 81.39.

6.4.2 From Table II for females, *AAD*(76) is 85.71.

6.4.3 I'll show Formula 6.5. $AAD(91) = 91 + .5 + (l_{92} + l_{93} + \ldots + l_{99})/l_{91} = 91.5 + 1{,}225{,}875/502{,}572 = 93.9392027411 \approx 93.94$.

6.4.4 We are looking for the age at which half the original cohort has died and half survived. Table II shows that $l_{80} = 5{,}056{,}025$ and $l_{81} = 4{,}722{,}378$, so the median is somewhere between 80 and 81, but closer to 80. In fact, 5,000,000 is about 17% of the way from 80 to 81 because (5,056,025 − 5,000,000)/(5,056,025 − 4,722,378) = 56,025/333,647 ≈ .168 = 16.8%.

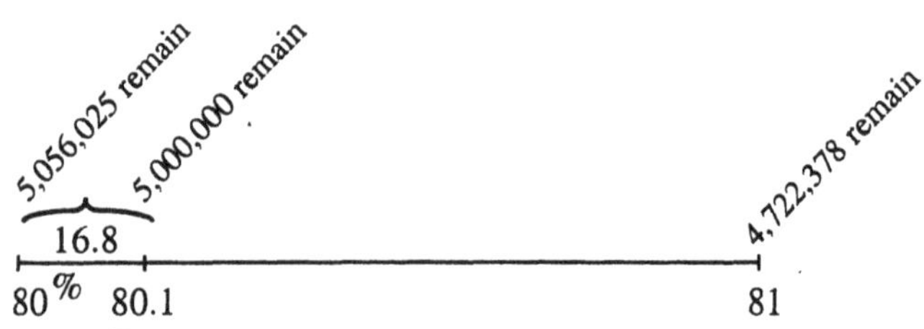

Time Diagram for Exercise 6.4.4

6.4.5 Since $l_{69} = 7{,}603{,}626$ and $l_{70} = 7{,}448{,}816$, Q_1 is between 69 and 70. By the same reasoning as in the preceding problem, Q_1 is about 67% of the way from 69 to 70, so $Q_1 = 69.67$. Similarly, since $l_{87} = 2{,}512{,}591$ and $l_{88} = 2{,}152.486$, and since 2,500,000 is about 3% of the way from 87 to 88, $Q_3 = 87.03$.

6.4.6 Formula 6.4 is:

$$AAD(x) = (x + .5)({}_{0|}q_x) + (x + 1.5)({}_{1|}q_x) +$$

$$(x + 2.5)({}_{2|}q_x) + \ldots + (99.5)({}_{99-x|}q_x).$$

This can first be written as

$$x\cdot {}_{0|}q_x + (x+1)({}_{1|}q_x) + (x+2)({}_{2|}q_x) + \ldots + (99)\,({}_{99-x|}q_x) +$$

$$(.5)({}_{0|}q_x + {}_{1|}q_x + {}_{2|}q_x + \ldots + {}_{99-x|}q_x) =$$

$$.5 + x\cdot {}_{0|}q_x + (x+1)({}_{1|}q_x) + (x+2)({}_{2|}q_x) + \ldots + (99)({}_{99-x|}q_x),$$

because, as we have seen before, ${}_{0|}q_x + {}_{1|}q_x + {}_{2|}q_x + \ldots + {}_{99-x|}q_x = 1$.

Now ${}_{t|}q_x = \dfrac{d_{x+t}}{l_x}$, so we rewrite once again

$$AAD(x) = .5 + \frac{x\cdot d_x + (x+1)\cdot d_{x+1} + (x+2)\cdot d_{x+2} + \ldots + 99\cdot d_{99}}{l_x}.$$

Using the facts that

a) $d_y = l_y - l_{y+1}$

and

b) $l_y = d_y + d_{y+1} + d_{y+2} + \ldots + d_{99}$,

we are going to rewrite

$$x\cdot d_x + (x+1)\cdot d_{x+1} + (x+2)\cdot d_{x+2} + \ldots + 99\cdot d_{99}.$$

We get

$$x\cdot d_x + (x+1)\cdot d_{x+1} + (x+2)\cdot d_{x+2} + \ldots + 99\cdot d_{99} =$$

$$x\cdot(d_x + d_{x+1} + d_{x+2} + \ldots + d_{99})$$

$$+ d_{x+1} + 2d_{x+2} + 3d_{x+3} + \ldots + (99-x)d_{99} =$$

$$x\cdot l_x + d_{x+1} + d_{x+2} + d_{x+3} + \ldots + d_{99} +$$

$$d_{x+2} + d_{x+3} + \ldots + d_{99} +$$

$$+ d_{x+3} + \ldots + d_{99} +$$

$$\ldots$$

$$d_{98} + d_{99} +$$

$$+ d_{99}$$

$$= x \cdot l_x + l_{x+1} + l_{x+2} + l_{x+3} + \ldots l_{99}.$$

Finally we can write

$$AAD(x) = .5 + \frac{x \cdot l_x + l_{x+1} + l_{x+2} + \ldots + l_{99}}{l_x} =$$

$$x + .5 + \frac{l_{x+1} + l_{x+2} + \ldots + l_{99}}{l_x},$$

which is Formula 6.5.

6.4.7 $AAD(21) = 77.10$ for females and 72.47 for males. The difference is 4.63 years.

6.4.8 A search of Tables I and II shows that the male partner should be around 25. $AAD(30) = 77.65$ for females while $AAD(25) =$ 72.84 for males, a difference of 4.81 years. Thus, a 25-year-old male and a 30-year-old female have about the same average remaining life. Of course, this just an average. In reality there would be very large variations from the averages.

6.4.9 We can use Formula 6.4 or 6.5. If you did Exercise 6.3.6, you calculated the probability distribution for the ages at death. These are {0.31732, 0.25651, 0.20242, 0.14675, 0.07700}. Formula 6.4 gives

$$AAD(95) = (95.5)(0.31732) + (96.5)(0.25651) +$$

$$(97.5)(0.20242) + (98.5)(0.14675) + (99.5)(0.07700)$$

$$\approx 96.91.$$

Using Formula 6.5, we get

$$AAD(95) = 95.5 + \frac{l_{96} + l_{97} + l_{98} + l_{99}}{l_{95}} = 95.5 + \frac{561{,}947}{398{,}655}$$

$$\approx 96.91,$$

the same as before. Note that this is also the value given in Table II.

Exercises 6.5

6.5.1 Possible causes for higher mortality in males between ages 11 and 28 are: higher risk of death during military service, reckless behavior such as driving too fast, drinking and driving, riding motorcycles, and similarly open vehicles without proper headgear, general feeling of immortality. Maybe you can think of some more, like homicide and suicide.

6.5.2 Using the approximation $\mu(x) \approx q_x$, we see from Table I that this is lowest at $x = 10$. That is the lowest q_x is $q_{10} = .00073$.

6.5.3 Using the approximation $\mu(x) \approx q_x$, we see from Table II that this is lowest at $x = 10$. That is the lowest q_x is $q_{10} = .00068$.

6.5.4 Formula 6.6 says that $\mu(x) \approx \frac{l_x - l_{x+t}}{t \cdot l_x}$ for small t. Note that in calculating the approximation, we can ignore the factor of 10,000,000 because it cancels out. This means that Formula 6.6 becomes

$$\mu(x) \approx \frac{(.933)^x - (.933)^{x+t}}{t \cdot (.933)^x} = \frac{1 - (.933)^t}{t}.$$

The right-hand side does not depend on the age x. We will get the same force of mortality for any age. If we evaluate this for $t = .1, .01$, and $.001$ in succession we get

$$\mu(x) \approx .06911 \text{ when } t = .1$$
$$\mu(x) \approx .06933 \text{ when } t = .01$$
$$\mu(x) \approx .06935 \text{ when } t = .001$$

Remark: The fact that the force of mortality in the above problem is the same for any age stems from the fact that the survival function is an exponential function--a function of the form $l_x = l_0 \cdot c^x$, where c is a constant between 0 and 1. An interesting consequence of having such a survival function is that the beings in the population it models do not age. This is not to say that they do not die. They just do not die from aging. While human populations do not have constant forces of mortality, certain electronic components have been found to have nearly constant forces of mortality.

6.5.5 When $t = 1$, $\frac{1 - {}_tp_x}{t} = 1 - {}_1p_x = {}_1q_x = \frac{d_x}{l_x} = q_x$ as claimed.

Miscellaneous Exercises – Chapter 6

6M1. The missing entries for l_x and d_x are found from the relationship $l_x - d_x = l_{x+1}$. Then $q_x = d_x/l_x$ and I would use Formula 6.5 to find $AAD(x)$.

x	l_x	d_x	q_x	$AAD(x)$
0	1,000	**600**	**0.6000**	**1.132**
1	**400**	255	**0.6375**	**2.080**
2	145	**87**	0.6000	**3.100**
3	**58**	**29**	0.5000	**4.000**
4	**29**	**29**	1.0000	**4.500**

For example $AAD(2) = 2 + .5 + \dfrac{l_3 + l_4}{l_2} = 2.5 + \dfrac{58+29}{145} = 3.10.$

6M2. Below are the results in a table:

x	l_x	d_x	q_x	$AAD(x)$
0	10,000	2,000	0.20	2.0104
1	8,000	3,200	0.40	2.3880
2	4,800	2,880	0.60	2.9800
3	1,920	1,536	0.80	3.7000
4	384	384	1.00	4.5000

6M3. On planet Q0317B, 66.5153846154; on Q0317C, 77.3159113673

6M4. $n = .47722181601$.

Chapter 7

Exercises 7.1

7.1.1 Here is a time diagram for Jean's life annuity:

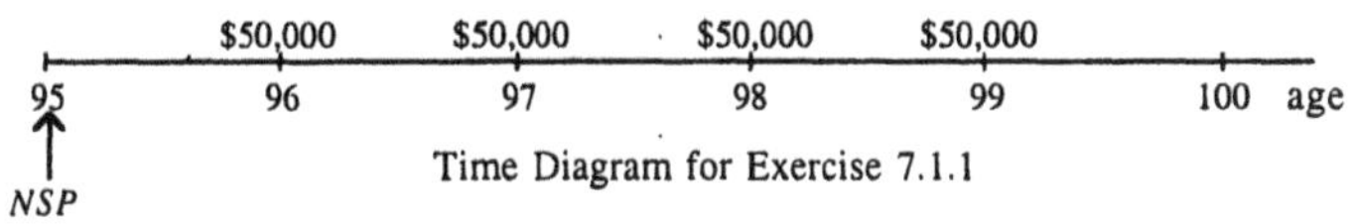

Time Diagram for Exercise 7.1.1

Jean's net single premium is

$$NSP = \$50{,}000(1.05)^{-1}{}_1p_{95} + \$50{,}000(1.05)^{-2}{}_2p_{95} +$$

$$\$50{,}000(1.05)^{-3}{}_3p_{95} + \$50{,}000(1.05)^{-4}{}_4p_{95} =$$

$$\$50{,}000\{(1.05)^{-1}l_{96} + (1.05)^{-2}l_{96} + (1.05)^{-3}l_{96} + (1.05)^{-4}l_{96}\}/l_{95} =$$

$$\$50{,}000(515{,}603.693317)/398{,}655 = \$64{,}667.91.$$

7.1.2 The same time diagram as that for Exercise 7.1.1 applies here, and Gene's net single premium is written the same way. It differs only in that we go to Table I for the l-values. We get

$$NSP = \$50{,}000(184{,}524.033607)/146{,}721 = \$62{,}882.63.$$

That Gene's *NSP* is lower than Jean's is to be expected. Gene pays a little less because he is not expected to get as many payments as Jean.

Exercises 7.2

7.2.1 a) In the time diagram below, I've put the arrow at age 60,

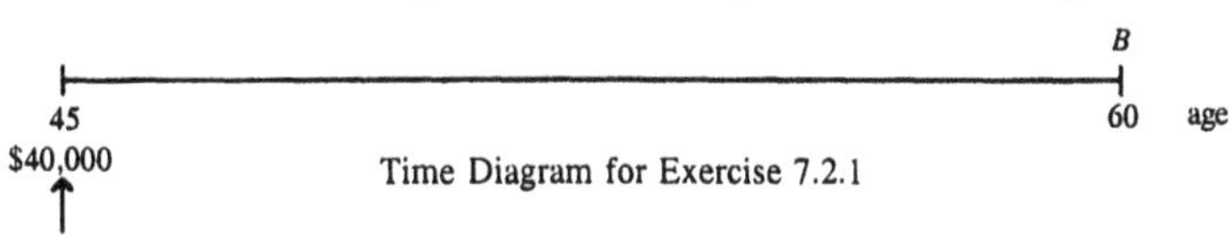

Time Diagram for Exercise 7.2.1

but I could just as well have put it at age 45 or anywhere else for that matter. The equation of value is

$$\$40{,}000 = B \cdot {}_{15}E_{45} = B \cdot \frac{D_{60}}{D_{45}} =$$

$$B \cdot \frac{613{,}356.44}{1{,}298{,}140.38} = B(.47248853009),$$

with $i = 4.5\%$, from which we arrive at $B = \$84{,}658.14$.

b) Here we change the interest rate to 6% and get $B =$ \$104,836.46.

7.2.2 a) This calls for Formula 1.2:

$$P = \$50{,}000(1.0375)^{-25} = \$19{,}918.99.$$

b) This is the present value of a 25-year pure endowment of \$50,000 to a man aged 20. Referring to Formula 7.3, $P =$

$$\$50{,}000\,{}_{25}E_{20} = \$50{,}000\frac{D_{45}}{D_{20}} = \$50{,}000\frac{1{,}757{,}148.70}{4{,}671{,}192.05}$$

$= \$18{,}808.35.$

7.2.3 a) Johanna will receive a 30-year pure endowment of B, where

$$B \cdot {}_{30}E_{30} = B\frac{D_{60}}{D_{30}} = \$100{,}000,$$

so

$$B = \$100{,}000\frac{D_{30}}{D_{60}} = \$603{,}715.54.$$

b) If Johanna or her estate were sure to receive the payment, the equation of value would be

$$B(1.0575)^{-30} = \$100{,}000,$$

or $B = \$100{,}000(1.0575)^{30} = \$535{,}070.84$

7.2.4 From the preceding problem, we know that $B = \$100{,}000\frac{D_{30}}{D_{60}}$,

so

$$B = \$100{,}000\frac{D_{30}}{D_{60}} = \$100{,}000 \cdot \frac{(1.0575)^{-30}10^7(1-\frac{30}{105})}{(1.0575)^{-60}10^7(1-\frac{60}{105})}$$

$= \$891{,}784.73.$

7.2.5 From the preceding two problems, we know that $B =$ $\$100{,}000\frac{D_{30}}{D_{60}}$, so

$$B = \$100{,}000\frac{D_{30}}{D_{60}} = \$100{,}000\cdot\frac{(1.0575)^{-30}10^7\sqrt{1-\frac{30}{105}}}{(1.0575)^{-60}10^7\sqrt{1-\frac{60}{105}}}$$

$$= \$690{,}773.48.$$

7.2.6 The net single premium for the annuity is

$$NSP = \$50{,}000\left(\frac{D_{96}}{D_{95}}+\frac{D_{97}}{D_{95}}+\frac{D_{98}}{D_{95}}+\frac{D_{99}}{D_{95}}\right) =$$

$$\$50{,}000\left(\frac{D_{96}+D_{97}+D_{98}+D_{99}}{D_{95}}\right).$$

This must be calculated from Table IV at 5%. The result is \$64,667.90. The slight discrepancy with Exercise 7.1.1 is due to round-off error.

7.2.7 The formula is the same as for the previous exercise, but we calculate from Table III and get \$62,882.72. The slight discrepancy with Exercise 7.1.2 is due to round-off error.

You expect the premium for females to be higher since they have lower mortality than males of the same age. On average they receive payments longer than a man of the same age.

7.2.8 Rong has bought a pure endowment of B with a net single premium of \$50,000. We are looking for B assuming $i = j_1 =$ 4.5%. The equation of value is

$$\$50{,}000 = B\cdot{}_{25}E_{35} = B\frac{D_{60}}{D_{35}}$$

$$= B\frac{613{,}356.44}{2{,}064{,}796.84} = B(.29705413536),$$

so $B = \$168{,}319.49$.

7.2.9 For most ages, it is the case that x-year-old females have a higher probability of surviving for another t years than x-year-old males do. You can observe this by making some calculations in the tables, but we cannot verify this mathematically. Put this information into the annuity formulas and you see that women would pay more than a man for the same annuity. This would not be the case if their mortality experiences were combined into a single table.

7.2.10 Each entry in the Table will be of the form $\$100{,}000\frac{D_{x+20}}{D_x}$.

$j_1\backslash x$	25	45	65
3%	\$52,773.57	\$44,062.67	\$13,162.37
5%	\$35,923.20	\$29,993.65	\$8,959.68
7%	\$24,631.19	\$20,565.52	\$6,143.32

7.2.11 Again, each entry in the Table will be of the form $\$100{,}000\frac{D_{x+20}}{D_x}$, but now we go to Table IV.

$j_1\backslash x$	25	45	65
3%	\$53,337.82	\$47,863.68	\$22,222.62
5%	\$36,307.26	\$32,581.02	\$15,127.04
7%	\$24,894.53	\$22,339.58	\$10,372.04

Exercises 7.3

7.3.1 The equation of value is

$$\$90{,}000 = P\frac{N_{50}}{D_{29}},$$

from which we find $P = \$90{,}000\frac{D_{29}}{N_{50}} = \$25{,}115.31$.

7.3.2 When Naomi is 55, her pension fund is worth

$$\$43{,}600\frac{N_{55}}{D_{55}} = \$636{,}416.71.$$

7.3.3 For this problem, we calculate $\$50{,}000\frac{N_{55}(i)}{N_{32}(i)-N_{55}(i)}$ for $i =$ .02, .03, …, .08. We have already done the calculations for $i =$ .06, .07 and .08. I have done the others and put them all in the table below:

i	0.02	0.03	0.04	0.05	0.06	0.07	0.08
P	\$27,266.14	\$21,579.54	\$17,157.49	\$13,698.39	\$10,977.92	\$8,827.87	\$7,121.05

Here is a graph of the annual payments versus the interest rate.

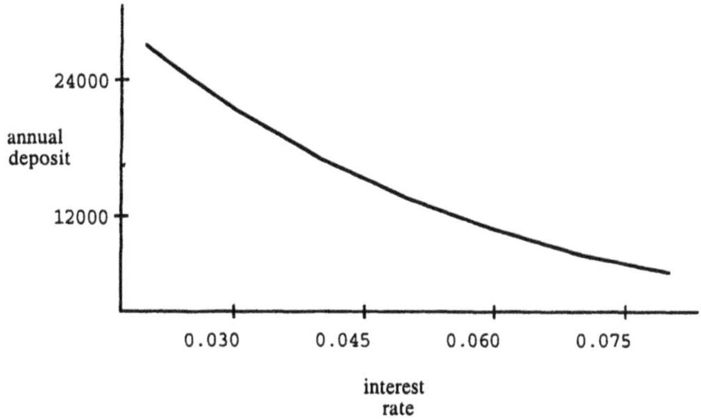

7.3.4 The equation of value for Sven's transaction is

$$\$250{,}000 = P\frac{N_{73}}{D_{72}} = P(7.17267361455),$$

so $P = \$34{,}854.51$.

7.3.5 For $35 \le x \le 65$ the x-th term of the forborne annuity, $\$5{,}000\frac{N_{35}-N_{65}}{D_{65}}$ is

$$\$5{,}000\frac{D_x}{D_{65}} = \$5{,}000(1.06)^{65-x}\frac{l_x}{l_{65}},$$

and each of these terms either exceed or equal $\$5{,}000(1.06)^{65-x}$ since the ratio $\frac{l_x}{l_{65}}$ exceeds or equals 1. On the other hand, for $35 \le x \le 65$, $\$5{,}000(1.06)^{65-x}$ is the x-th term of the 30-year annuity certain of \$5,000 at 6%. This means that term by term the forborne annuity exceeds the annuity certain, so the sum of the terms of the forborne annuity exceed the sum of the terms of the annuity certain.

7.3.6 The time diagram below describes Elena's annuity. Her net

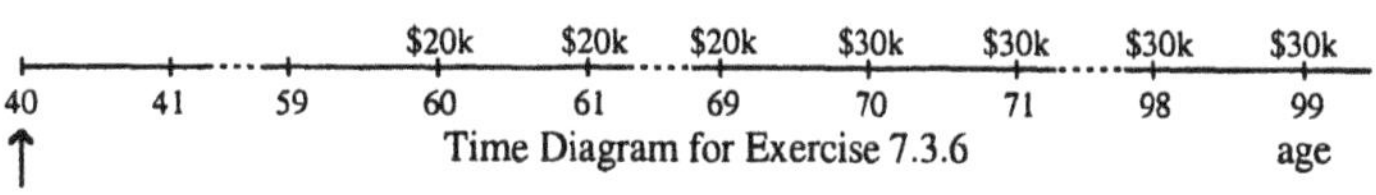

Time Diagram for Exercise 7.3.6

single premium is

$$NSP = \$20{,}000\frac{N_{60} - N_{70}}{D_{40}} + \$30{,}000\frac{N_{70}}{D_{40}} =$$

$$\$10{,}000\frac{2N_{60} + N_{70}}{D_{40}} = \$79{,}644.10.$$

7.3.7 I have added 20 payments of P to the time diagram of the preceding problem.

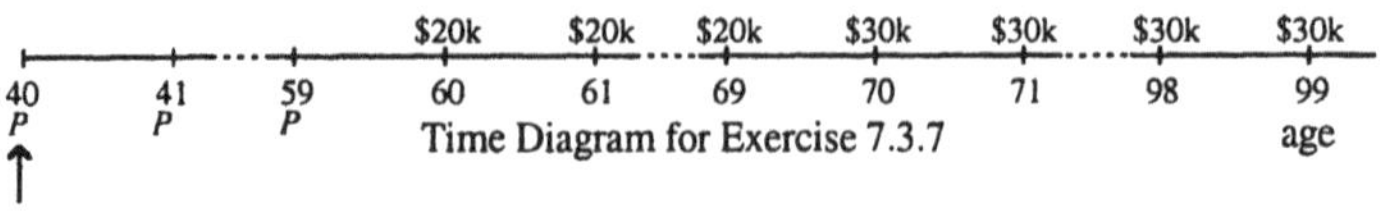

Time Diagram for Exercise 7.3.7

The equation of value is

$$P\frac{N_{40} - N_{60}}{D_{40}} = \$10{,}000\frac{2N_{60} + N_{70}}{D_{40}},$$

and solving this for P gives

$$P = \$10{,}000\frac{2N_{60} + N_{70}}{N_{40} - N_{60}} = \$6{,}740.18.$$

You may have noticed that we could have used the numerical result from the preceding problem to solve this one. The reason that I went through the algebra is to make the next problem easier.

7.3.8 From Exercises 7.3.6 and 7.3.7 we have the formulas:

$$NSP = \$10{,}000\frac{2N_{60} + N_{70}}{D_{40}},$$

and

$$NAP = P = \$10{,}000\frac{2N_{60} + N_{70}}{N_{40} - N_{60}}$$

Using Table IV with $i = 3\%$, we get $NSP = \$192{,}072.41$ and $NAP = \$12{,}952.04$.

7.3.9 The two are identical except for the first payment of \$50,000 immediately. It is not necessary to calculate the values of the two annuities. Thus, the difference between the two is \$50,000.

7.3.10 We use Formula 7.6 twice in this problem. We see that the value of Rodica's contributions to her pension have present value

$$P\frac{N_{31}-N_{65}}{D_{31}}=P\frac{39{,}046{,}202.41-3{,}919{,}749.18}{2{,}136{,}271.62}$$

$$=P(16.4428778163).$$

The present value of the pension of \$80,000 annually beginning at age 65 is

$$\$80{,}000\frac{N_{65}}{D_{31}}=\$80{,}000\frac{3{,}919{,}749.18}{2{,}136{,}271.61}=\$146{,}788.42.$$

Setting the two present values equal, we get P = \$146,788.42/16.4428778163 = \$8,927.17.

7.3.11 With the help of the time diagram

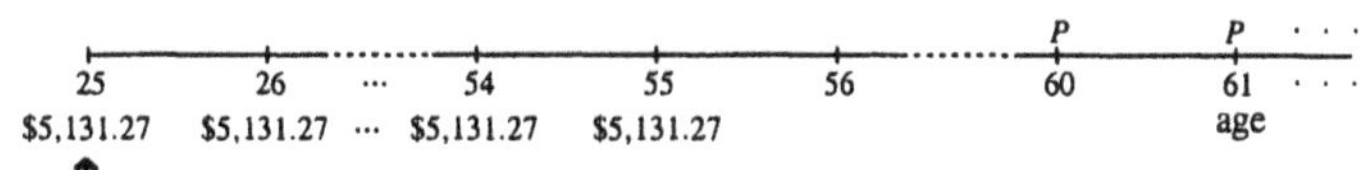

Time Diagram for Exercise 7.3.11

we can write an equation of value

$$\$5{,}131.27\frac{N_{25}-N_{56}}{D_{25}}=P\frac{N_{60}}{D_{25}}.$$

The solution, using Table III, with $i=.055$ is

$$P=\$5{,}131.27\frac{N_{25}-N_{56}}{N_{60}}=\$54{,}836.05.$$

7.3.12 The time diagram helps us write the equation of value

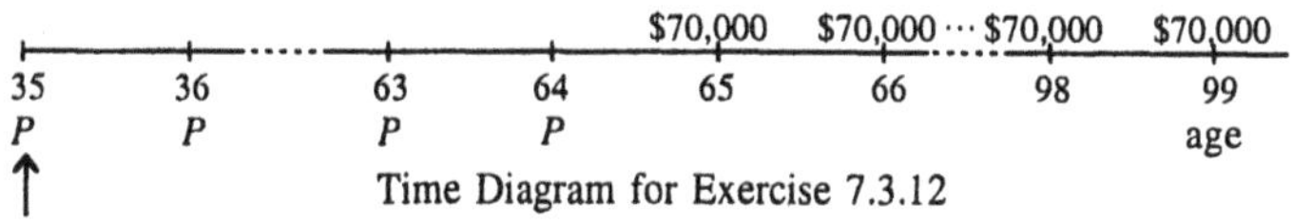

Time Diagram for Exercise 7.3.12

$$P\frac{N_{35}-N_{65}}{D_{35}}=\$70{,}000\frac{N_{65}}{D_{35}},$$

and using Table IV with $i=4.75\%$ we get

$$P = \$70{,}000 \frac{N_{65}}{N_{35} - N_{65}} = \$10{,}767.30.$$

7.3.13 The net single premium is

$$NSP = \$30{,}000 \frac{N_{35}(i)}{D_{35}(i)},$$

for i = .04, .05 and .06. Using Table III, the respective solutions are \$587,477.36, \$514,357.55 and \$456,061.59.

7.3.14 The net single premiums should be higher for women since they are expected to live longer. They receive payments longer, on average. As in the preceding problem, the net single premium is written

$$NSP = \$30{,}000 \frac{N_{35}(i)}{D_{35}(i)},$$

this time using Table IV for i = .04, .05 and .06. The respective solutions are \$615,488.24, \$534,172.23 and \$470,307.71

Exercises 7.4

7.4.1 Use Formula 7.7 with inputs

$P = \$43{,}000,$
$x = a = c = 60,$
$i = .0675,$
$k = .0338983,$
$i^* = (i - k)/(1 + k) = .0325,$
gender = *female*,
and $b = 100$.

We calculate

$$\hat{S}^{(.0338...)} = \$43{,}000 \frac{N_{60}(.0325)}{D_{60}(.0325)} \frac{D_{60}(.0675)}{D_{60}(.0675)} = \$655{,}057.20.$$

7.4.2 Use Formula 7.7 with inputs

$P = \$10{,}000,$
$x = 30,$
$i = .06,$
$k = .0291262,$

$i^* = (i - k)/(1 + k) = .03$,
gender = *male*,
$a = 40$,
$b = 60$,
and $c = 30$.

Manu's net single premium is

$$NSP = \hat{S}^{(.0291...)} = \$10{,}000\frac{N_{40}(.03) - N_{60}(.03)}{D_{40}(.03)}\frac{D_{40}(.06)}{D_{30}(.06)}$$

$$= \$80{,}203.72.$$

7.4.3 We are given that $i^* = 0$ and $a = c$. When we substitute these into Formula 7.7, we get

$$\hat{S}^{(k)} = P\frac{N_a(0) - N_b(0)}{D_a(0)}.$$

Using the definitions of D and N with $i^* = 0$, we next write

$$\hat{S}^{(k)} = P\frac{l_a + l_{a+1} + \ldots + l_{b-1}}{l_a} =$$

$$P\frac{(l_a + l_{a+1} + \ldots + l_{99}) - (l_b + l_{b+1} + \ldots + l_{99})}{l_a} =$$

$$P\left\{\frac{l_a + l_{a+1} + \ldots + l_{99}}{l_a} - \frac{l_b}{l_a}\left(\frac{l_b + l_{b+1} + \ldots + l_{99}}{l_b}\right)\right\} =$$

$$P\left\{\left(a + \frac{1}{2} + \frac{l_{a+1} + \ldots + l_{99}}{l_a} + \frac{1}{2} - a\right) - \frac{l_b}{l_a}\left(b + \frac{1}{2} + \frac{l_{b+1} + \ldots + l_{99}}{l_b} + \frac{1}{2} - b\right)\right\}$$

$$= P\left\{\left(AAD(a) + \frac{1}{2} - a\right) - \frac{l_b}{l_a}\left(AAD(b) + \frac{1}{2} - b\right)\right\}.$$

This last expression confirms Formula 7.8.

7.4.4 We will use Formula 7.7 with inputs

$P = \$6{,}400$,
$x = 23$,
$i = .055$,

$k = .0343137255,$
$i^* = (i - k)/(1 + k) = .02,$
gender = *male*,
$a = 24,$
$b = 66,$
and $c = 65.$

The result is

$$\hat{S}^{(.03431...)} = \$6,400 \frac{N_{24}(.02) - N_{66}(.02)}{D_{24}(.02)} \frac{D_{24}(.055)}{D_{65}(.055)}$$

$$= \$2,061,709.12.$$

7.4.5 Here we have $i^* = 0$, $a = c = 22$, $b = 66$, and $B = \$32,000$. From Formula 7.8 we calculate

$$\hat{S}^{(.03)} = \$32,000 \left\{ \frac{1}{2} + AAD(22) - 22 - \frac{l_{66}}{l_{22}} \left(\frac{1}{2} + AAD(66) - 66 \right) \right\}$$

$$= \$1,310,000$$

to the nearest \$10,000.

7.4.6 We need to add the expected retirement income to what we found in the preceding exercise. Now we have $i^* = 0$, $a = 66$, $b = 100$, $c = 22$, and $B = \$32,000(1.03)^{42}(.75) = \$83,056.70$. From Formula 7.8 and the remark following it, we have the expected retirement income of

$$\hat{S}^{(.03)} = \$83,056.70 \left(\frac{1}{2} + AAD(66) - 66 \right) \left(\frac{D_{66}(.03)}{D_{22}(.03)} \right)$$

$$= \$231,000.$$

Note that the second term in Formula 7.8 vanishes because $l_{100} = 0$. Combining the last result with the result of Exercise 7.5.5, the widow should be trying to recover \$1,541,000.

7.4.7 Magnus's retirement income forms an increasing life annuity. The inputs to Formula 7.7 are $P = \$80,000$, $x = 32$, $a = 60$, $b = 100$, $c = 32$, $i = .065$, $k = .03398058$, $i^* = .03$, and $g = male$. The value of Magnus's retirement income when he is 32 is

$$\hat{S}^{(.03398...)} = \$80{,}000\frac{N_{60}(.03)}{D_{60}(.03)}\frac{D_{60}(.065)}{D_{32}(.065)} =$$

$$\$80{,}000\frac{18{,}504{,}969.74}{1{,}372{,}167.45}\cdot\frac{184{,}783.90}{1{,}272{,}483.82} = \$156{,}669.02.$$

7.4.8 Csilla will contribute to an increasing life annuity with inputs $x = 27$, P is to be determined, $g = female$, $k = .033816425$, $i = .07$, $i^* = .035$, $a = 28$, $b = 65$, and $c = 65$. In addition, we are given that $\hat{S}^{(.033816...)} = \$1{,}000{,}000$. The equation of value is

$$\$1{,}000{,}000 = P\frac{N_{28}(.035) - N_{65}(.035)}{D_{28}(.035)}\frac{D_{28}(.07)}{D_{65}(.07)}$$

$$= P(300.159432802),$$

so $P = \$3{,}331.56$. Csilla's last payment at age 64 will be $P(1.0338\ldots)^{36} = \$11{,}030.91$.

7.4.9 The inputs for Formula 7.7 are $x = 50$, $P = \$50{,}000$, g = female, $k = 3\%$, $i = 5.5\%$, $i^* = (.055 - .03)/(1.03) = 0.02427184466$, $a = 55$, $b = 99$, and $c = 50$. We need to evaluate

$$\hat{S}^{(.03)} = \$50{,}000\frac{N_{55}(0.02427...)}{D_{55}(0.02427...)}\frac{D_{55}(.055)}{D_{50}(.055)}.$$

We do not have a table for $i = .02427...$ The idea here is for you to generate a spreadsheet to find $N_{55}(0.02427...)$ and $D_{55}(0.02427...)$. I will not reproduce that spreadsheet here, but the result we sought is $\hat{S}^{(.03)} = \$50{,}000\cdot(18.7964323563)\cdot(.74340248857) = \$698{,}665.73$.

Miscellaneous Exercises – Chapter 7

7M1. a) The present value of the first 15 payments to Arvind is, from Formula 3.2,

$$S(\$75{,}000, .0225, 15, -32) = \$474{,}556.6983.$$

The contingent part of Arvind's annuity has present value

$$\hat{S} = \$75{,}000\frac{N_{75}}{D_{28}} = \$104{,}934.55655.$$

The entire premium is $474,556.6983 + $104,934.55655 =

$579,491.25.

b) Here, the present value of the first 15 payments to Arvind is, from Formula 3.2,

$$S(\$75{,}000, .0775, 15, -32) = \$64{,}451.1273.$$

The contingent part of Arvind's annuity has present value

$$\hat{S} = \$75{,}000\frac{N_{75}}{D_{28}} = \$7{,}003.6656.$$

The entire premium is $64,451.1273 + $7,003.6656 = $71,454.79.

c) Arvind pays less in b) because his premium grows at a faster rate.

7M2. Let B denote the size of Nelly's pure endowment at age 65. Then its present value is

$$B\cdot {}_{40}E_{25} = B\frac{D_{65}}{D_{25}}.$$

The present value of Nelly's $1,000 payments is

$$\hat{S} = \$1{,}000\frac{N_{25} - N_{65}}{D_{25}}.$$

Setting these two equal and solving for B, and referring to Table IV with $i = 6.75\%$, we get

$$B = \$1{,}000\frac{N_{25} - N_{65}}{D_{65}} = \$234{,}255.99.$$

7M3. If all payments were certain, Nelly's 'endowment-certain' would be

$$S(\$1{,}000, .0675, 40, 40) = \$199{,}850.08.$$

7M4. We can use Formula 7.7 with inputs

$$P = \$35{,}000,$$

$x = 35,$
$i = .06,$
$k = .0291262,$
$i^* = (i - k)/(1 + k) = .03,$

gender = *male*,
$a = 35$,
$b = 100$,
and $c = 35$.

Our estimate is

$$\hat{S}^{(0291...)} = \$35,000\frac{N_{35}(.03)}{D_{35}(.03)} = \$35,000\frac{76,529,520.62}{3,373,196.51}$$

$$= \$794,063.79.$$

7M5. The net single premium on all three planets can be written

$$\hat{S} = \$10,000\frac{N_{35}}{D_{35}}.$$

For the Earth-woman, we use Table IV with $i = 5\%$ and find $\hat{S}$ = \$178,057.41. For the other two women, we have to take apart $\hat{S}$:

$$\hat{S} = \$10,000\frac{N_{35}}{D_{35}} = \$10,000\frac{D_{35} + D_{35} + D_{35} + ... + D_{99}}{D_{35}}.$$

Next we note that

$$D_x = (1.05)^{-x} l_x.$$

Now we can evaluate $\hat{S}$ using a spreadsheet or other program. When I did this, I got \$148,095.00 for the Q0317B-woman and \$169,532.61 for the Q0317C-woman.

Chapter 8

Exercises 8.2

8.2.1 The formula for the net single premium is

$$I = \$200{,}000\frac{M_{35}(i)}{D_{35}(i)},$$

for $i = .04$, .05 and .06. From Table III we find a) \$49,364.78, b) \$36,711.89, and c)\$27,901.29.

8.2.2 As in the preceding problem, the formula for the net single premium is

$$I = \$200{,}000\frac{M_{35}(i)}{D_{35}(i)},$$

for $i = .04$, .05 and .06, but this time we use Table IV. We find a) \$42,182.50, b) \$30,421.51, and c) \$22,525.39.

8.2.3 In general the net single premiums for life annuities decrease as the interest rate increases. Also, women pay more than men for the same level of annuity because they are expected to receive more payments.

The net single premium for a whole-life insurance policy decreases as the interest rate increases. Women pay less than men for the same level of insurance because the benefit will likely be paid later than for men of the same age at purchase.

8.2.4 We have

$$M_{96} = 37{,}805(1.02375)^{-97} + 29{,}054(1.02375)^{-98}$$

$$+ 20{,}693(1.02375)^{-99} + 10{,}757(1.02375)^{-100} = 9{,}845.91216486\ldots$$

8.2.5 Using Table III we get the following:

		Interest Rate (i)		
		3%	5%	7%
Age (x)	**30**	\$29,832.26	\$15,045.14	\$8,403.63
	50	\$48,971.53	\$32,524.11	\$22,704.69
	70	\$72,602.97	\$60,078.65	\$50,565.89

Net Single Premiums for Males for Exercise 8.2.5

8.2.6 Dmitrij should pay the net single premium

$$I = 4{,}365{,}000\frac{M_{37}}{D_{37}}\text{ RUR} = 867{,}706.24\text{ RUR}.$$

8.2.7 Dmitrij should pay the net annual premium

$$NAP = 4{,}365{,}000\frac{M_{37}}{N_{37}}\text{ RUR} = 51{,}571.00\text{ RUR}.$$

8.2.8 Given the lower mortality of women, they tend to pay less than men for the same level of life insurance because the insurance company pays benefits at a later age to women than to men, on average.

Exercises 8.3

8.3.1 Linda will pay

$$I = \$150{,}000\frac{M_{36}(.05) - M_{65}(.05)}{D_{36}(.05)} = \$9{,}794.15.$$

8.3.2 The time diagram below shows the elements of the problem.

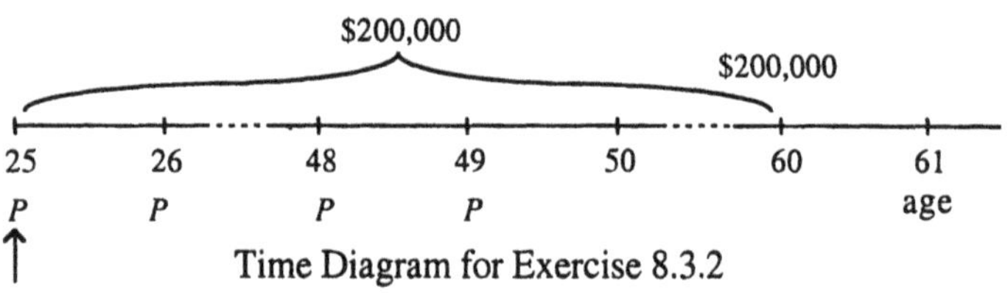

Time Diagram for Exercise 8.3.2

The equation of value is

$$P\frac{N_{25} - N_{50}}{D_{25}} = \$200{,}000\frac{M_{25} - M_{60} + D_{60}}{D_{25}}.$$

Solving for P gives

$$P = \$200{,}000\frac{M_{25} - M_{60} + D_{60}}{N_{25} - N_{50}} = \$3{,}510.17.$$

8.3.3 Adelaida's net single premium looks like this:

$$NSP = I = \$1{,}000{,}000\frac{M_{25}(i) - M_{26}(i)}{D_{25}(i)},$$

for i = .02, .04, .06, and .08. Using Table IV, here are the results in a table:

i	2%	4%	6%	8%
$NSP(i)$	\$1,137.25	\$1,115.38	\$1,094.33	\$1,074.07

8.3.4 Pierre's net single premium looks like Adelaida's, but we use Table III:

$$NSP = I = \$1{,}000{,}000\frac{M_{25}(i) - M_{26}(i)}{D_{25}(i)},$$

for i = .02, .04, .06, and .08. Using Table III, here are the results in a table:

i	2%	4%	6%	8%
$NSP(i)$	\$1,735.34	\$1,701.97	\$1,669.86	\$1,638.93

8.3.5 Eva's equation of value is

$$\$1{,}000\frac{N_{25} - N_{45}}{D_{25}} = B\frac{M_{25} - M_{55}}{D_{25}},$$

which, when solved for B yields

$$B = \$1{,}000\frac{N_{25} - N_{45}}{M_{25} - M_{55}} = \$380{,}463.21.$$

8.3.6 We can write an equation of value:

$$\$1{,}200\frac{N_{35} - N_{65}}{D_{35}} = \frac{\$100{,}000(M_{35} - M_{65}) + B \cdot D_{65}}{D_{35}}.$$

Solving this equation for B gives Sarafino's endowment:

$$B = \frac{\$1{,}200(N_{35} - N_{65}) - \$100{,}000(M_{35} - M_{65})}{D_{65}} = \$67{,}970.16.$$

8.3.7 A time diagram and equation of value for Elliot's term insurance and life annuity are given below:

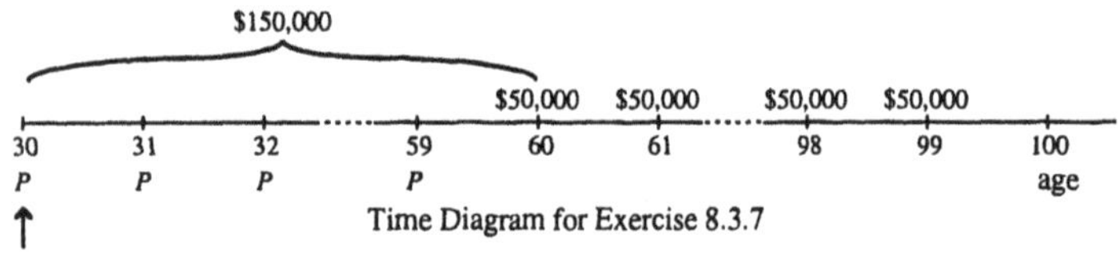

Time Diagram for Exercise 8.3.7

$$P\frac{N_{30}-N_{60}}{D_{30}}=\$150{,}000\frac{M_{30}-M_{60}}{D_{30}}+\$50{,}000\frac{N_{60}}{D_{30}},$$

which implies that Elliot's 30 annual premiums will be

$$P=\frac{\$150{,}000(M_{30}-M_{60})+\$50{,}000N_{60}}{N_{30}-N_{60}}=\$6{,}866.17.$$

8.3.8 a) Kai's net single premium is

$$NSP=I=\$200{,}000\frac{M_{27}}{D_{27}}=\$26{,}631.42.$$

b) Kai's net annual premium is the solution for P of the equation of value

$$P\frac{N_{27}-N_{60}}{D_{27}}=\$200{,}000\frac{M_{27}}{D_{27}}.$$

Using Table IV, we get

$$P=\$200{,}000\frac{M_{27}}{N_{27}-N_{60}}=\$1{,}536.70.$$

8.3.9 The net single premium is

$$NSP=I=\$100{,}000\frac{M_x-M_{x+1}}{D_x};$$

for $x = 30, 40, 50, 60, 70, 80,$ and 90. See the Table below:

Age	*Net Single Premium (Males)*	*Net Single Premium (Females)*
30	$164.76	$128.57
40	$287.62	$230.48
50	$639.05	$472.38
60	$1,531.43	$901.90
70	$3,762.86	$2,105.71
80	$9,413.34	$6,284.76
90	$21,120.89	$18,166.69

Net Single Premiums at 5% for Males & Females, Ages 30 to 90 In Steps of 10

8.3.10 The equation of value for a $100,000 whole-life policy for (50) is

$$P\frac{N_{50}}{D_{50}} = \$100,000\frac{M_{50}}{D_{50}},$$

which has the solution

$$NAP = P = \$100,000\frac{M_{50}}{N_{50}}.$$

This is evaluated for interest rates 2% through 8% in the table below:

%	*Net Annual Premium (Males)*	*Net Annual Premium (Females)*
2	$3,104.44	$2,548.81
3	$2,795.21	$2,240.14
4	$2,527.18	$1,977.98
5	$2,295.29	$1,756.27
6	$2,094.87	$1,569.30
7	$1,921.66	$1,411.89
8	$1,771.85	$1,279.40

Net Annual Premiums for 50-Year Old Males & Females, i=2% to 8%

8.3.11 a) The equation of value for the endowment insurance is

$$\$27{,}500 = B\frac{M_{27} - M_{60} + D_{60}}{D_{27}} = B(.23599997533),$$

so $B = \$116{,}525.44$.

b) Without the endowment portion the equation of value becomes

$$\$27{,}500 = B\frac{M_{27} - M_{60}}{D_{27}} = B(.04507917895)$$

so that $B = \$610{,}037.73$.

8.3.12 With the help of the time diagram below, we see that the present value of the insurance at age a is

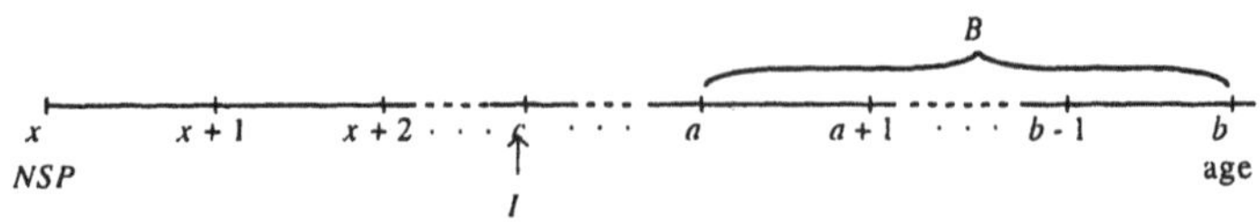

Time Diagram for Formula 8.3

$$B\{{}_{0|}q_a(1+i)^{-1} + {}_{1|}q_a(1+i)^{-2} + \ldots + {}_{b-a-1|}q_a(1+i)^{-(b-a)}\} =$$

$$B\frac{d_a(1+i)^{-1} + d_{a+1}(1+i)^{-2} + \ldots + d_{b-1}(1+i)^{-(b-a)}}{l_a} =$$

$$B\frac{d_a(1+i)^{-(a+1)} + d_{a+1}(1+i)^{-(a+2)} + \ldots + d_{b-1}(1+i)^{-b}}{l_a(1+i)^{-a}} =$$

$$B\frac{M_a - M_b}{D_a}.$$

To find the value the insurance at age c, we accumulate or discount the previous value according to whether $c < a$ or $c > a$. We do this using Formula 7.4. In this case, the factor is D_a/D_c. The value of the insurance at age c is therefore

$$I = B\frac{M_a - M_b}{D_a}\frac{D_a}{D_c} = B\frac{M_a - M_b}{D_c}.$$

If $b = 100$, $M_b = 0$ and this gives the reduction indicated in Formula 8.3.

Exercises 8.4

8.4.1 Melinda's equal annual premiums from age 35 to aged 59 have present value

$$\$950\frac{N_{35}(.065)-N_{60}(.065)}{D_{35}(.065)} = \$12{,}028.4731781.$$

Using Formula 8.8 with inputs $a = c = x = 35$, B (to be determined), $g = female$, $k = .0390244$, $i = .065$, $i^* = (i-k)/(1+k) = .025$, and $b = 100$, the present value of her increasing insurance is

$$I^{(.0390...)} = B\frac{M_{35}(.025)}{D_{35}(.025)}\frac{D_{35}(.065)}{D_{35}(.065)} = B\frac{M_{35}(.025)}{D_{35}(.025)}$$

$$= B(.3614348999).$$

Setting the two present values equal and solving for B, we find $B = \$33{,}279.78$.

8.4.2 For the net single premium, we want to use Formula 8.8 with inputs $a = c = x = 40$, $B = \$125{,}000$, $g = male$, $k = .03$, $i = .055$, $i^* = (i-k)/(1+k) = .02427184466$, and $b = 65$. The net single premium is

$$I^{(.03)} = \$125{,}000\frac{M_{40}(.02427...)-M_{65}(.02427...)}{D_{40}(.02427...)}\frac{D_{40}(.055)}{D_{40}(.055)} =$$

$$\$125{,}000\frac{M_{40}(.02427...)-M_{65}(.02427...)}{D_{40}(.02427...)}$$

$i^* = .02427184466$ is 70.87...% of the way from .0225 to .025, so we will take as our approximation, the amount 70.87...% of the way from $I^{(k)}$ evaluated at .0225 to $I^{(k)}$ evaluated at .025. At $i^* = .0225$, we get $I^{(k)} = \$19{,}028.5873599$. At $i^* = .025$, $I^{(k)} = \$18{,}315.6281145$. The value 70.87...% from the former to the latter is $I^{(k)} = \$18{,}523.29$.

We also need Lonny's net annual premium. Its present value is

$$P\frac{N_{40}(.055)-N_{65}(.055)}{D_{40}(.055)}=P(13.4198825395),$$

giving $P =$ \$18,523.29/13.4198825395 = \$1,380.29.

8.4.3 The time diagram below suggests that we write Peter's net single premium as

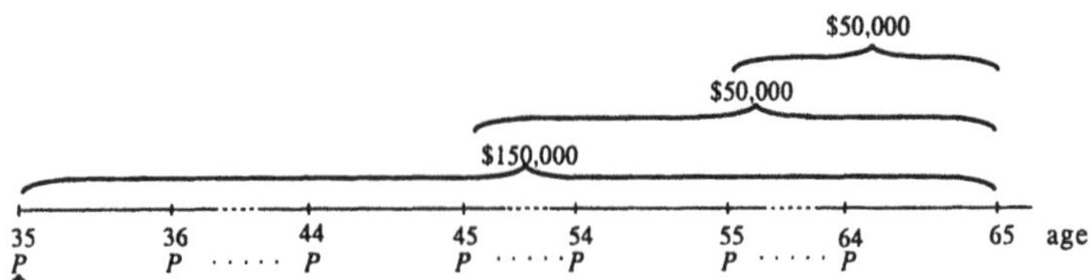

Figure 8.10--Time Diagram for Exercise 16

$$NSP=\$150{,}000\frac{M_{35}-M_{65}}{D_{35}}+\$50{,}000\frac{M_{45}-M_{65}}{D_{35}}$$

$$+\ \$50{,}000\frac{M_{55}-M_{65}}{D_{35}}.$$

We can rewrite this as

$$\frac{\$150{,}000M_{35}+\$50{,}000M_{45}+\$50{,}000M_{55}-\$250{,}000M_{65}}{D_{35}},$$

We do not need to go on because this last expression matches the expression we found in Example 8.14.

8.4.4 a) Ziad's benefit if he died at 79 would be

$$\$50{,}000(1.04411764706)^{50}=\$432{,}954.05.$$

b) Noting that $i^* = (.065 - .04411764706)/1.04411765 = .02$, and using Formula 8.8, Ziad's net single premium would be

$$NSP=I^{(.0441...)}=\$50{,}000\frac{M_{30}(.02)}{D_{30}(02)}\frac{D_{30}(.065)}{D_{30}(065)}=$$

$$\$50{,}000\frac{M_{30}(.02)}{D_{30}(02)}=\$21{,}805.09.$$

c) Ziad's net annual premium P satisfies

$$P\frac{N_{30}(.065)}{D_{30}(.065)} = \$21{,}805.09.$$

This leads to

$$P = \$21{,}805.09\frac{D_{30}(.065)}{N_{30}(.065)} = \$1{,}472.62.$$

8.4.5 a) The net single premium for the fixed benefit of \$50,000 is

$$NSP_1 = \$50{,}000\frac{M_{25}(.045)}{D_{25}(.045)} = \$7{,}411.687.$$

The net single premium for the decreasing benefit requires Formula 8.8 with $i^* = (.045 + .027904)/(1 - .027904) = .075$. This premium is

$$NSP_2 = \$50{,}000\frac{M_{25}(.075) - M_{55}(.075)}{D_{25}(.075)}\frac{D_{25}(.045)}{D_{25}(.045)}$$

$$= \$1{,}546.826.$$

Lars's net single premium is \$7,411.687 + \$1,546.826 = \$8,958.51.

b) We set $\$8{,}958.51 = P\dfrac{N_{25}(.045) - N_{55}(.045)}{D_{25}(.045)}$ and solve for P, getting $P = \$540.40$.

8.4.6 The net single premium for the insurance evaluated at age a is

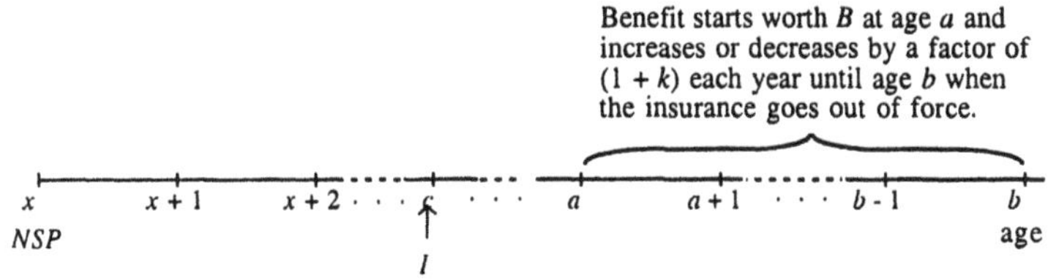

Time Diagram for Formula 8.8

$$B\{{}_{0|}q_a(1+k)(1+i)^{-1} + {}_{1|}q_a(1+k)^2(1+i)^{-2} + \cdots$$

$$+ {}_{b-a-1|}q_a(1+k)^{b-a}(1+i)^{-(b-a)}\}.$$

As before I have written the net single premium as a weighted average. In this case it is the weighted average of the benefits, $B(1+k)$, $B(1+k)^2$, $B(1+k)^3$, …, $B(1+k)^{b-a}$ with weights ${}_{t|}q_a$, $t = 0, 1, \ldots, b-a-1$.

Now, replace each factor of $(1+k)(1+i)^{-1}$ by $(1+i^*)^{-1}$, write each ${}_{t|}q_a$ as $\frac{d_{a+t}}{l_a}$, and gather terms to get:

$$B\frac{d_a(1+i^*)^{-1}+d_{a+1}(1+i^*)^{-2}+\ldots+d_{b-1}(1+i^*)^{-(b-a)}}{l_a} =$$

$$B\frac{d_a(1+i^*)^{-(a+1)}+d_{a+1}(1+i^*)^{-(a+2)}+\ldots+d_{b-1}(1+i^*)^{-b}}{(1+i^*)^{-a}l_a} =$$

$$B\frac{M_a(i^*)-M_b(i^*)}{D_a(i^*)}.$$

Here, I have used the definitions of the commutation functions M and D. To evaluate this insurance at age c we multiply by the accumulation/discount factor $D_a(i)/D_c(i)$ to get

$$I^{(k)} = B\frac{M_a(i^*)-M_b(i^*)}{D_a(i^*)}\frac{D_a(i)}{D_c(i)}.$$

8.4.7 From the derivation in the preceding exercise, we see that when $i^* = 0$ we can write

$$I^{(k)} = B\frac{M_a(i^*)-M_b(i^*)}{D_a(i^*)}\frac{D_a(i)}{D_c(i)} =$$

$$B\left(\frac{d_a+d_{a+1}+\ldots+d_{b-1}}{l_a}\right)\left(\frac{D_a(i)}{D_c(i)}\right) = B\left(\frac{l_a-l_b}{l_a}\right)\left(\frac{D_a(i)}{D_c(i)}\right).$$

When $a = c$, the second factor is equal to 1 and need not be written.

8.4.8 We have $i^* = 0$, $a = c = 35$, $b = 55$, and $B = \$250{,}000$. With the aid of the result of the previous exercise, we find Adelle's net single premium to be

$$I^{(.04)} = \$250{,}000\frac{l_{35}-l_{55}}{l_{35}} = \$17{,}636.04.$$

Adelle's equal annual payments of P satisfy the equation

$$P\frac{N_{35}(.04)-N_{55}(.04)}{D_{35}(.04)}=P(13.7469115311)=\$17{,}636.04,$$

so that P = \$1,282.91.

Miscellaneous Exercises – Chapter 8

8.M.1 Gabriella's net single premium can be written

$$I=Q(i)=\$100{,}000\frac{M_{30}(i)}{D_{30}(i)}.$$

We estimate the rate of change in I by

$$\frac{Q(4.25\%)-Q(3.75\%)}{4.25\%-3.75\%}=$$

$$\frac{\$16{,}271.40884-\$19{,}627.38759}{4.25\%-3.75\%}=$$

$$\text{-}\$6{,}711.96$$

per 1% increase in the interest rate when $i = 4\%$.

8.M.2 The net single premium for the insurance is

$$I=Q(i)=\$100{,}000\frac{M_{30}(i)}{D_{30}(i)}$$

We estimate the rate of change in I by

$$\frac{Q(5.25\%)-Q(4.75\%)}{5.25\%-4.75\%}=$$

$$\frac{\$11.440.54112-\$13{,}591.62558}{5.25\%-4.75\%}=$$

$$\text{-}\$4{,}302.17$$

per 1% increase in the interest rate when $i = 5\%$.

The only difference between this and the preceding problem is the interest rate. Evidently the rate of change in the net single premium for this insurance is increasing as i increases.

8.M.3 With $i^* = (.075 - .043689\ldots)/1.043689\ldots = .03$, the equation of value is

$$\$8{,}000\frac{N_{30}(.03)-N_{60}(.03)}{D_{30}(.03)}\frac{D_{30}(.075)}{D_{30}(.075)}=$$

$$\$250{,}000\frac{M_{30}(.03)-M_{60}(.03)}{D_{30}(.03)}\frac{D_{30}(.075)}{D_{30}(.075)}+$$

$$P\frac{N_{60}(.03)}{D_{60}(.03)}\frac{D_{60}(.075)}{D_{30}(.075)}.$$

Solving for P, we get $P = \$102{,}635.77$.

8.M.4 (🖳) The net single premium on all three planets takes the form

$$NSP=\$100{,}000\frac{M_{35}}{D_{35}}.$$

For the earthling, we can use Table IV with $i = 5\%$ to get

$$NSP_{Earth} = \$15{,}210.76.$$

For the other two we need to use the definitions of M and D with their particular survival functions. To evaluate the premiums you need a spreadsheet program or some other program able to evaluate long sums. I have done this with a spreadsheet and gotten

$$NSP_{\text{Q0317B}} = \$32{,}500.12,$$

and

$$NSP_{\text{Q0317C}} = \$21{,}245.38.$$

Chapter 9

Exercises 9.2

9.2.1 A time diagram will help to determine the annual premium:

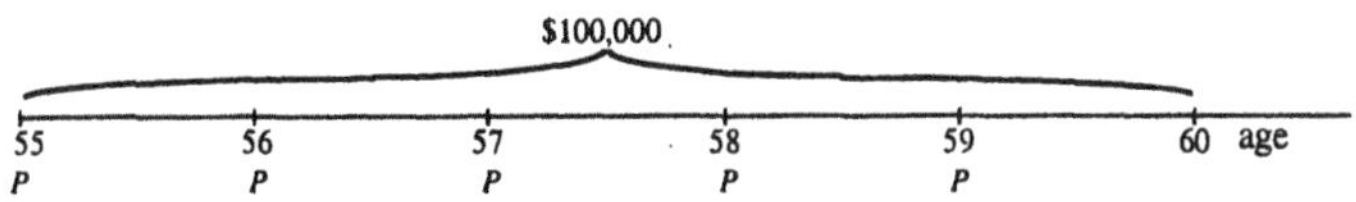

Time Diagram for Exercise 9.2.1

Using Formulas 7.6 and 8.3, the net annual premium satisfies the equation

$$P\frac{N_{55}-N_{60}}{D_{55}}=\$100,000\frac{M_{55}-M_{60}}{D_{55}},$$

so

$$P=\$100,000\frac{M_{55}-M_{60}}{N_{55}-N_{60}}=\$1,193.3912241002$$

$$\approx \$1,193.39.$$

Following the pattern of Table 9.2, and using Table III with i = 4.25%, we get the following table:

Yr	*Premiums*	*Beginning-of Year Fund*	*Fund Plus Interest*	*No. of Deaths*	*End-of-Year fund*	*No. of Survivors*	*Reserve/ Policy*
1	10,276,936,262	10,276,936,262	10,713,706,053	90,163	1,697,406,053	8,521,377	$199.19
2	10,169,336,529	11,866,742,582	12,371,079,142	97,655	2,605,579,142	8,423,722	$309.31
3	10,052,795,909	12,658,375,051	13,196,355,991	105,212	2,675,155,991	8,318,510	$321.59
4	9,927,236,832	12,602,392,822	13,137,994,517	113,049	1,833,094,517	8,205,461	$223.40
5	9,792,325,147	11,625,419,664	12,119,500,000	121,195	0	8,084,266	$0.00

Table for Exercise 9.2.1

Notice that the reserve per policy at the end of the fifth year is $0, as it should be.

9.2.2 The time diagram for this exercise differs from the previous one only by the payment of $100,000 to the insured, if he survives to age 60.

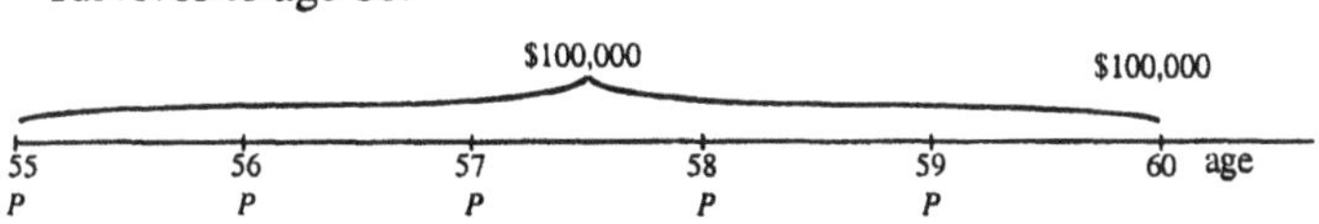

Time Diagram for Exercise 9.2.2

The equation for the net annual premium is now

$$P\frac{N_{55}-N_{60}}{D_{55}}=\$100,000\frac{M_{55}-M_{60}+D_{60}}{D_{55}},$$

so

$$P=\$100,000\frac{M_{55}-M_{60}+D_{60}}{N_{55}-N_{60}}=\$18,103.379725117\approx\$18,103.38.$$

Yr	Premiums	Beginning-of Year Fund	Fund Plus Interest	No. of Deaths	End-of-Year fund	No. of Survivors	Reserve/ Policy
1	155,897,978,638	155,897,978,638	162,523,642,730	90,163	153,507,342,730	8,521,377	$18,014.38
2	154,265,723,612	307,773,066,342	320,853,421,662	97,655	311,087,921,662	8,423,722	$36,929.98
3	152,497,838,065	463,585,759,726	483,288,154,515	105,212	472,766,954,515	8,318,510	$56,833.13
4	150,593,145,277	623,360,099,792	649,852,904,033	113,049	638,548,004,033	8,205,461	$77,819.88
5	148,546,576,303	787,094,580,336	820,546,100,000	121,195	808,426,600,000	8,084,266	$100,000.00

Table for Exercise 9.2.2

Notice that the reserve per policy in the fifth year is $100,000--sufficient to pay the endowment.

9.2.3 We already know from Example 9.2 that Martina's net annual premium is P = $7,067.94464105. With the help of the time diagram in Figure 9.1, and thinking retrospectively, we can write the tth reserve as

$$R_t=\begin{cases}P\dfrac{N_{30}-N_{30+t}}{D_{30+t}}-\$100,000\dfrac{M_{30}-M_{30+t}}{D_{30+t}}, & 1\le t\le 5\\[2ex] P\dfrac{N_{30}-N_{35}}{D_{30+t}}-\$100,000\dfrac{M_{30}-M_{30+t}}{D_{30+t}}, & 6\le t\le 10\end{cases}$$

I used a spreadsheet program to generate a table and found a table identical to Table 9.3.

9.2.4 In Example 9.5 we found P = $21,195.7247920833 ≈ $21,195.72 . Using Figure 9.2 as a guide, we can write the prospective reserves as

$$R_t=\begin{cases}\$25,000\dfrac{N_{65}-N_{71}}{D_{60+t}}-P\dfrac{N_{60+t}-N_{65}}{D_{60+t}}, & 1\le t\le 4\\[2ex] \$25,000\dfrac{N_{60+t}-N_{71}}{D_{60+t}}, & 5\le t\le 10\end{cases}$$

Again, I used a spreadsheet program, and I duplicated Table 9.4.

9.2.5 Here is a time diagram for this policy:

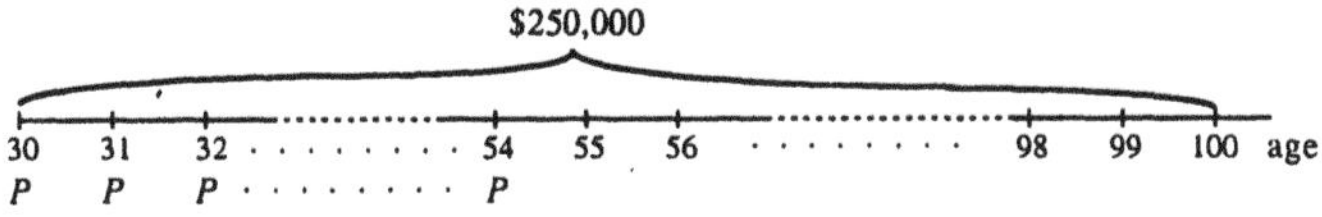

Time Diagram for Exercise 9.2.5

We calculate her annual premium with i = 6% from the equation

$$P\frac{N_{30}-N_{55}}{D_{30}} = \$250{,}000\frac{M_{30}}{D_{30}},$$

and get

$$P = \$250{,}000\frac{M_{30}}{N_{30}-N_{55}} = \$1{,}630.71133885$$

$$\approx \$1{,}630.71.$$

Now, looking at the time diagram, and thinking retrospectively, we get

$$R_{15} = P\frac{N_{30}-N_{45}}{D_{45}} - \$250{,}000\frac{M_{30}-M_{45}}{D_{45}}$$

$$= \$29{,}650.06.$$

9.2.6 Using the time diagram and payment amount found above, we can write the 15th reserve prospectively as

$$R_{15} = \$250{,}000\frac{M_{45}}{D_{45}} - P\frac{N_{45}-N_{55}}{D_{45}} = \$29{,}650.06,$$

as we found retrospectively.

9.2.7 Here is a time diagram:

Time Diagram for Exercise 9.2.7

The equation of value giving us his annual payments is

$$P\frac{N_{40}-N_{55}}{D_{40}}=\$75{,}000\frac{N_{60}}{D_{40}},$$

so, at $i = 5.5\%$,

$$P=\$75{,}000\frac{N_{60}}{N_{40}-N_{55}}=\$23{,}689.06.$$

With the help of the time diagram, and thinking retrospectively, we write

$$R_{10}=P\frac{N_{40}-N_{50}}{D_{50}}=\$331{,}407.97,$$

and

$$R_{30}=P\frac{N_{40}-N_{55}}{D_{70}}-\$75{,}000\frac{N_{60}-N_{70}}{D_{70}}=\$612{,}034.18.$$

9.2.8 We can use the same time diagram and value of P as in Exercise 9.2.7. This time, we think prospectively, and get

$$R_{10}=\$75{,}000\frac{N_{60}}{D_{50}}-P\frac{N_{50}-N_{55}}{D_{50}}=\$331{,}407.97,$$

and

$$R_{30}=\$75{,}000\frac{N_{70}}{D_{70}}=\$612{,}034.18,$$

just as we got retrospectively.

9.2.9 From the time diagram below we can write down the tth retrospective and prospective reserves:

$$RR_t=P\frac{N_x-N_{x+t}}{D_{x+t}}-B\frac{M_x-M_{x+t}}{D_{x+t}},$$

and

$$PR_t=B\frac{M_{x+t}}{D_{x+t}}-P\frac{N_{x+t}}{D_{x+t}},$$

where $P=B\cdot\frac{M_x}{N_x}$. This means that we need to show that

$$B\cdot\frac{M_x}{N_x}\cdot\frac{N_x-N_{x+t}}{D_{x+t}}-B\frac{M_x-M_{x+t}}{D_{x+t}}=B\frac{M_{x+t}}{D_{x+t}}-B\cdot\frac{M_x}{N_x}\cdot\frac{N_{x+t}}{D_{x+t}}.$$

Transposing gives

$$B\cdot\frac{M_x}{N_x}\cdot\frac{N_x-N_{x+t}}{D_{x+t}}+B\cdot\frac{M_x}{N_x}\cdot\frac{N_{x+t}}{D_{x+t}}=B\frac{M_{x+t}}{D_{x+t}}+B\frac{M_x-M_{x+t}}{D_{x+t}},$$

or

$$\frac{B\cdot M_x\cdot N_x-B\cdot M_x\cdot N_{x+t}+B\cdot M_x\cdot N_{x+t}}{N_x\cdot D_{x+t}}$$

$$=\frac{B\cdot M_{x+t}+B\cdot M_x-B\cdot M_{x+t}}{D_{x+t}}.$$

Canceling where we can gives

$$\frac{B\cdot M_x}{D_{x+t}}=\frac{B\cdot M_x}{D_{x+t}},$$

Which is certainly true, so $RR_t = PR_t$.

9.2.10 What we need to show is

$$RR_t = VPP_t - VPB_t = VFB_t - VFP_t = PR_t,$$

or, after transposing,

$$VPP_t + VFP_t = VFB_t + VPB_t.$$

What this says in its present form is that the value of all premiums is equal to the value of all benefits t years after issue. Then, discounting t years with interest and survivorship gives

$$(VPP_t + VFP_t)\cdot{}_tE_x = (VFB_t + VPB_t)\cdot{}_tE_x,$$

which states that the value of all premiums is equal to the value of all benefits at issue. This is the basic principle of equations of value.

Exercises 9.3

9.3.1 The time diagrams for the net and gross transactions, respectively, look like this:

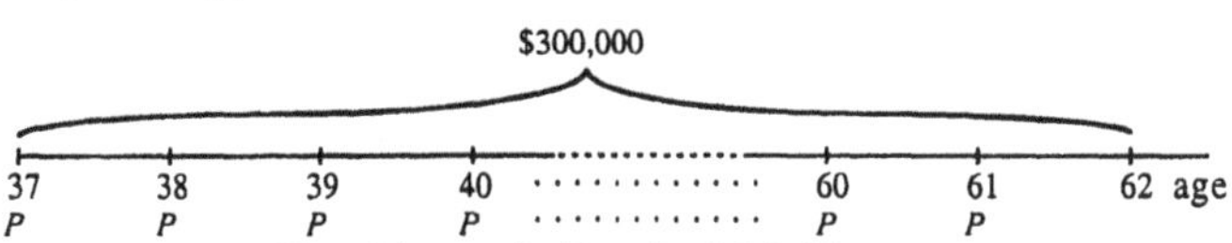

Time Diagram for Exercise 9.3.1 (Net)

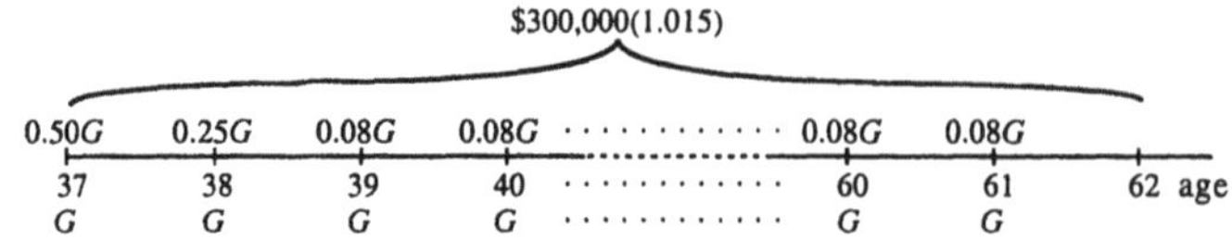

Time Diagram for Exercise 9.3.1 (Gross)

The equation of value for the net transaction is

$$P\frac{N_{37}-N_{62}}{D_{37}}=\$300{,}000\frac{M_{37}-M_{62}}{D_{37}},$$

or

$$P=\$300{,}000\frac{M_{37}-M_{62}}{N_{37}-N_{62}}=\$1{,}890.56.$$

On the other hand, the equation of value for the gross transaction can be written

$$G\frac{N_{37}-N_{62}}{D_{37}}=\$300{,}000(1.015)\frac{M_{37}-M_{62}}{D_{37}}+0.42G+$$

$$0.17G\frac{N_{38}-N_{39}}{D_{37}}+0.08G\frac{N_{37}-N_{62}}{D_{37}}.$$

The solution for G is

$$G=\frac{\$304{,}500(M_{37}-M_{62})}{0.92(N_{37}-N_{62})-0.42D_{37}-0.17(N_{38}-N_{39})}=\$2{,}166.40.$$

9.3.2 a)

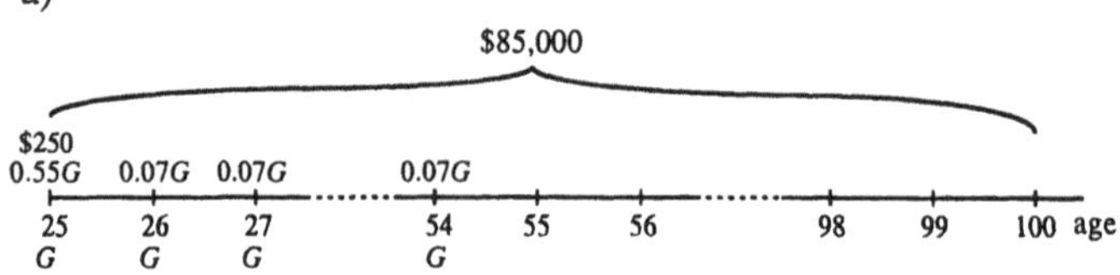

Time Diagram for Exercise 9.3.2a

With the help of the time diagram above, we can write an equation of value:

$$G\frac{N_{25}-N_{55}}{D_{25}}=\$85{,}000\frac{M_{25}}{D_{25}}+\$250+0.48G+0.07G\frac{N_{25}-N_{55}}{D_{25}}.$$

Solving for G, we get

$$G = \frac{\$85,000M_{25} + \$250D_{25}}{0.93(N_{25} - N_{55}) - 0.48D_{25}} = \$1,208.17.$$

b) Let's look at a time diagram for the net annual premium:

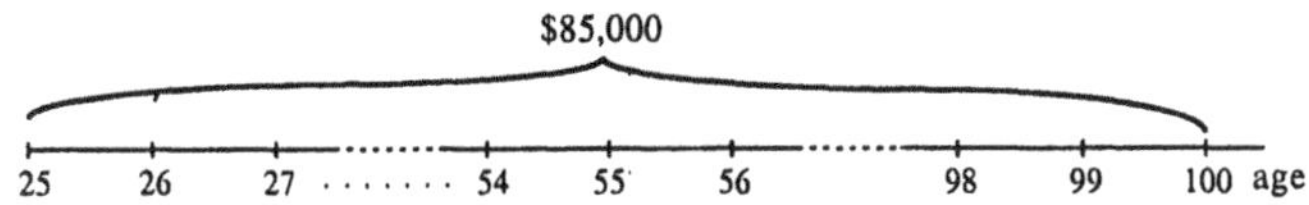

Time Diagram for Exercise 9.3.2b

The equation of value is

$$P\frac{N_{25} - N_{55}}{D_{25}} = \$85,000\frac{M_{25}}{D_{25}},$$

so that

$$P = \$85,000\frac{M_{25}}{N_{25} - N_{55}} = \$1,082.78.$$

9.3.3 Here is a time diagram for Devean's policy:

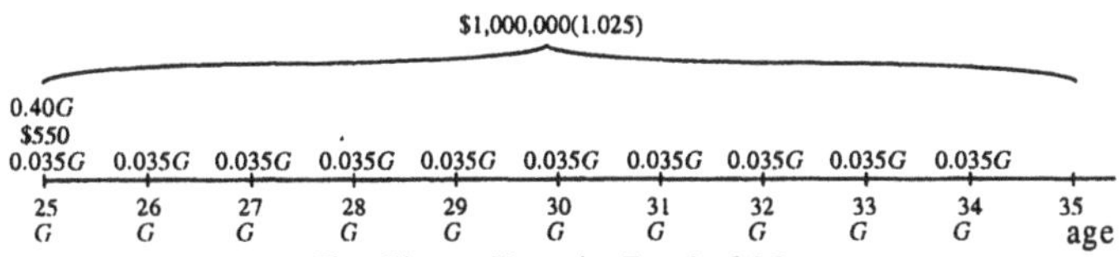

Time Diagram Illustrating Exercise 9.3.3

From the diagram we can write the equation of value.

$$G\frac{N_{25} - N_{35}}{D_{25}} = \$1,000,000(1.025)\frac{M_{25} - M_{35}}{D_{25}} + 0.40G + \$550 +$$

$$+ 0.035G\frac{N_{25} - N_{35}}{D_{25}}.$$

We get

$$G = \frac{\$1,025,000(M_{25} - M_{35}) + \$550D_{25}}{0.965(N_{25} - N_{35}) - 0.40D_{25}} = \$1,982.97.$$

9.3.4 Here is a time diagram:

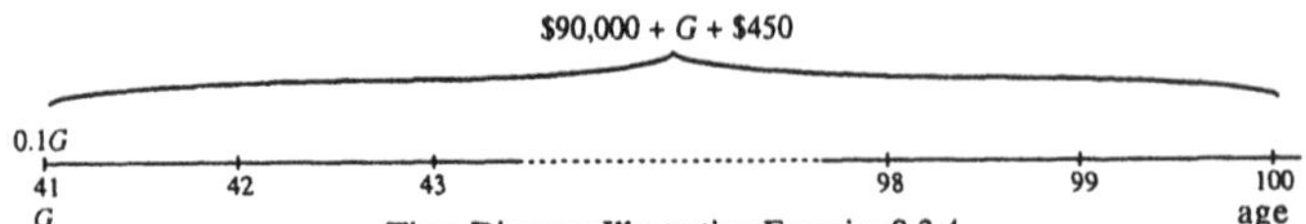

Time Diagram Illustrating Exercise 9.3.4

From this diagram we write the equation of value:

$$G = (\$90,450 + G)\frac{M_{41}}{D_{41}} + 0.1G.$$

When we solve this for G, we get

$$G = \frac{\$90,450 M_{41}}{0.9D_{41} - M_{41}} = \$89,294.21.$$

Remark: This is a very high premium, but, remember: It is returned as part of the benefit.

9.3.5 The time diagram below should illuminate the situation:

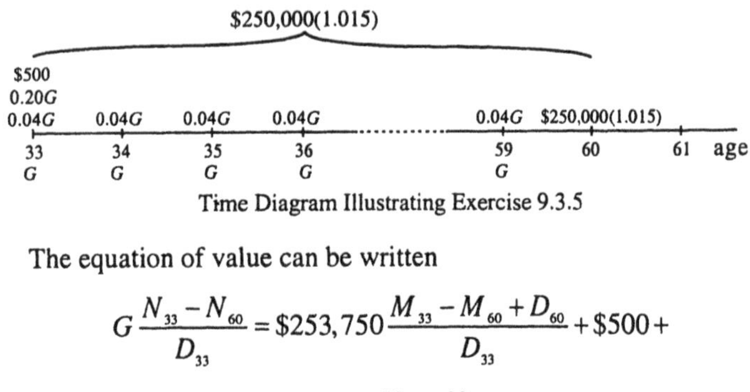

Time Diagram Illustrating Exercise 9.3.5

The equation of value can be written

$$G\frac{N_{33} - N_{60}}{D_{33}} = \$253,750\frac{M_{33} - M_{60} + D_{60}}{D_{33}} + \$500 +$$

$$0.20G + 0.04G\frac{N_{33} - N_{60}}{D_{33}},$$

which we solve for G to get

$$G = \frac{\$500D_{33} + \$253,750(M_{33} - M_{60} + D_{60})}{0.96(N_{33} - N_{60}) - 0.20D_{33}} = \$6,179.92.$$

9.3.6 Below is a time diagram for Mauricio's annuity:

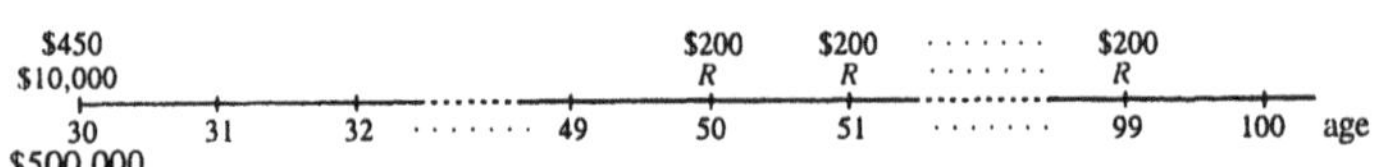

Time Diagram Illustrating Exercise 9.3.6

Mauricio's gross premium is \$500,000, so the 2% commission is \$10,000. We let R stand for the amount of Mauricio's annuity. An equation of value for the problem is

$$\$500{,}000 = \$10{,}450 + (R + \$200)\frac{N_{50}}{D_{30}}.$$

The solution for R is

$$R = \$489{,}550\frac{D_{30}}{N_{50}} - \$200 = \$97{,}738.14.$$

9.3.7 First, let's look at a time diagram:

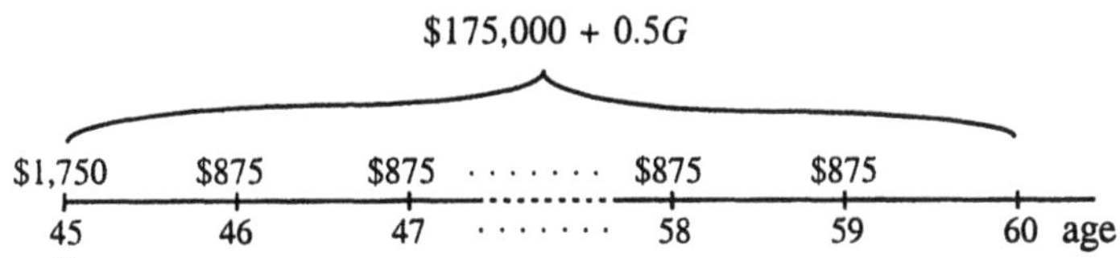

Time Diagram Illustrating Exercise 9.3.7

We can write down an equation directly:

$$G = (\$175{,}000 + 0.5G)\frac{M_{45} - M_{60}}{D_{45}} + \$875 + \$875\frac{N_{45} - N_{60}}{D_{45}},$$

and solve for G to get

$$G = \frac{\$875D_{45} + \$875(N_{45} - N_{60}) + \$175{,}000(M_{45} - M_{60})}{D_{45} - 0.5(M_{45} - M_{60})}$$

$$= \$21{,}978.01.$$

9.3.8 Consider the time diagram for Liam's policy:

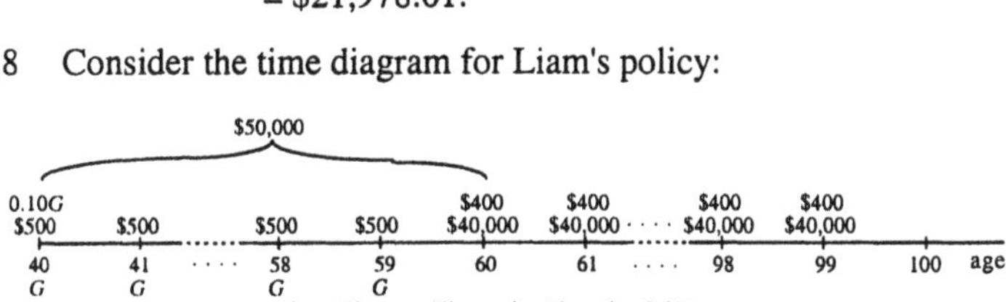

Time Diagram Illustrating Exercise 9.3.8

The equation of value may be written

$$G\frac{N_{40} - N_{60}}{D_{40}} = \$50{,}000\frac{M_{40} - M_{60}}{D_{40}} + 0.10G +$$

$$\$500\frac{N_{40}-N_{60}}{D_{40}}+\$40,400\frac{N_{60}}{D_{40}}.$$

We solve this equation for G and find

$$G=\frac{\$50,000(M_{40}-M_{60})+\$500(N_{40}-N_{60})+\$40,400N_{60}}{(N_{40}-N_{60})-0.1D_{40}}$$

$$=\$11,746.81.$$

9.3.9 Here is a time diagram for this annuity:

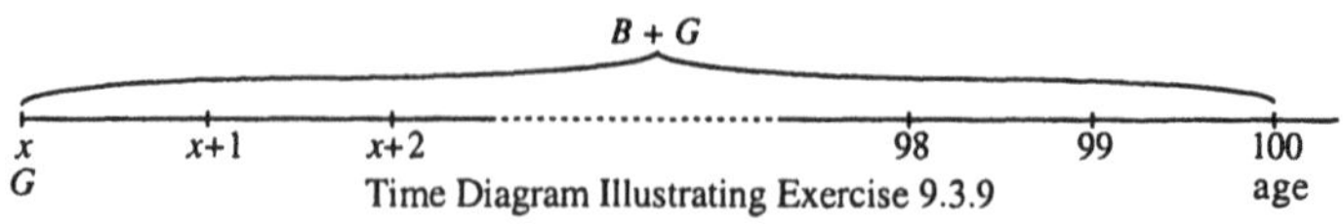

Time Diagram Illustrating Exercise 9.3.9

On the one hand, the net single premium, P, must satisfy

$$P=(B+G)\frac{M_x}{D_x}.$$

On the other hand, Formula 9.5 dictates that

$$G=(P+c)(1+k).$$

We have two equations in two unknowns, we get

$$G=\frac{(BM_x+cD_x)(1+k)}{D_x-M_x(1+k)}$$

9.3.10 The equation of value for this annuity is

$$G=(R+c)\frac{N_x}{D_x}+pG,$$

so

$$G=\frac{(R+c)N_x}{(1-p)D_x}.$$

9.3.11 We will use a time diagram here. In the diagram, we let j = 0.02926829268, and k = 0.03178484108, giving rise to the two values i_1^* = (0.055 - 0.02926829268)/1.02926829268 = 0.025, and i_2^* = (0.055 - 0.03178484108)/1.03178484108 = 0.0225 needed as inputs to Formula 7.7.

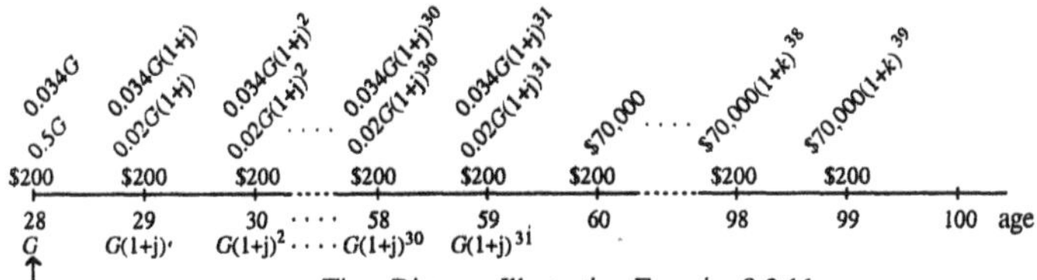

Time Diagram Illustrating Exercise 9.3.11

From the time diagram, and with the help of Formulas 7.6 and 7.7, we can deduce the equation of value:

$$G\frac{N_{28}(0.025)-N_{60}(0.025)}{D_{28}(0.025)}=\$200\frac{N_{28}(0.055)}{D_{28}(0.055)}+0.48G+$$

$$0.054G\frac{N_{28}(0.025)-N_{60}(0.025)}{D_{28}(0.025)}$$

$$+\ \$70{,}000\frac{N_{60}(0.0225)}{D_{60}(0.0225)}\frac{D_{60}(0.055)}{D_{28}(0.055)}.$$

Solved for G, we get

$$G=\frac{\$200\dfrac{N_{28}(0.055)}{D_{28}(0.055)}+\$70{,}000\dfrac{N_{60}(0.0225)D_{60}(0.055)}{D_{60}(0.0225)D_{28}(0.055)}}{0.946\dfrac{N_{28}(0.025)-N_{60}(0.025)}{D_{28}(0.025)}-0.48}$$

$$=\$6{,}361.38.$$

In a similar manner, we find Edsger's net annual premium to be

$$G=\$70{,}000\frac{\dfrac{N_{60}(0.0225)D_{60}(0.055)}{D_{60}(0.0225)D_{28}(0.055)}}{\dfrac{N_{28}(0.025)-N_{60}(0.025)}{D_{28}(0.025)}}=\$5{,}775.01.$$

www.ingramcontent.com/pod-product-compliance
Ingram Content Group UK Ltd.
Pitfield, Milton Keynes, MK11 3LW, UK
UKHW040227290926
15471UKWH00001B/43

9 780761 826231